The Russian Museum

A PICTORIAL GUIDE

You have entered the rooms of the Russian Museum. Outside, beyond the walls of the palace, there has remained the noisy city. In the palace you find yourselves in the realm of calm and silence — a calm of museum suites, a silence of paintings, sculptures and drawings. But are they really silent?

The museum can be compared to a giant theatre and its rooms to the stage where a grand performance is under way. Like a usual performance this pageant of art is built up of numerous mise-en-scenes — only here they are arrested for ever (or probably for a moment?) in thousands of pictures, statues and engravings.

Look at them closely — and you will discern the well-known theatrical genres: tragedy, drama, comedy and pastoral. And literary forms can be identified quite easily too: novels, stories, novellas, poems and sonnets.

Listen to them attentively — and you will make another rewarding discovery: artists and their characters address to you from the depth of time speaking the language of the visual arts.

The plasticity of gestures and poses of the people depicted, the harmony or dissonance of lines, volumes, colours and structures of simple or complex patterns and ornaments — all these and many other nuances form together what is called the style in art.

Every age has a distinctive style of its own, its favourite motifs, melodies, tunes and rhythms, its special sense of space and time. Learning to recognize and differentiate them you open in yourselves an access to the spiritual riches accumulated by our predecessors.

It is this opportunity to overcome the invisible wall of time, to make a pilgrimage to the past, to sense one's personal relation to history that attracts people to the museum. And so as to prevent you from getting lost on this exciting tour, we have tried to supply it with required landmarks and guidelines. As a result we offer you this art book — a guide to the Russian Museum.

Vladimir Gusev,
Director of the Russian Museum

The State Staircase of the Alexander III Russian Museum
1900. Photograph

THE MIKHAILOVSKY PALACE

History of the Palace
The Creation of the Museum

St Petersburg, the city founded in 1703 at the will of Emperor Peter the Great, is pervaded with imperial grandeur even today. Its palaces and architectural ensembles are marked by rare integrity and austere, haunting beauty. One of precious gems in this architectural treasury is the Mikhailovsky Palace. Nowadays it houses the world's largest museum of Russian fine arts. The museum is relatively young — it is a little more than one hundred years old, and the palace itself is much older.

The palace's first owner was Grand Duke Mikhail Pavlovich, the fourth, youngest son of Emperor Paul I (hence the name of the building — the Mikhailovsky Palace). In 1798, soon after the grand duke's birth, the Emperor ordered to put annually several hundred thousand roubles aside to construct for him in the future the palace that would correspond in its luxury and comfort to the grandeur and tastes of the imperial family. When the accumulated sum reached nine million roubles and Grand Duke Mikhail was in his early twenties, the construction of the palace began.

The palace was designed and built by the outstanding architect Carlo Rossi (1777–1849). The ensemble of the Mikhailovsky Palace was created by Rossi in the prime of his architectural career — between 1819 and 1825. As usual, the architect not only solved the task of putting up a separate building, but he designed its environment too. Rossi worked out projects for the construction of dwelling houses to shape the new, Mikhailovsky Square (now Arts Square), laid new streets opening up two strikingly thought-out vistas — one formal, affording a view of the southern palatial façade from Nevsky Prospect and the other, more romantic street, unfolding from the Field of Mars towards the northern front of the Mikhailovsky Palace which faces the garden. Maybe this front is less famous, but by no means less interesting and splendid.

There are perhaps not very many surviving architectural monuments which so perfectly and fully epitomize the highest accomplishments of the Empire style in Russia and even all over Europe as the Mikhailovsky Palace. "This palace is undoubtedly a triumph of the newest architecture… It not only surpasses all seen at the Tuileries and other royal palaces on the continent, but is positively unique in its own right," wrote an Englishman on a visit Russia in 1826 (A. V. Polovtsov, *A Tour around the Russian Museum of Emperor Alexander III in St Petersburg*, Moscow, 1900, pp. 5–6).

The outer appearance of the main building and the western wing have survived to the present day practically with no alterations, but only some interiors can give us a full idea of the architect's original project and his outstanding talent. The imposing main vestibule with a wide staircase which forks into two flights of stairs leading to the gallery of the first floor with eighteen grandiose Corinthian columns and the suite of rooms running along the perimeter of the ground floor. Its centre is the White Hall notable for the commensurate proportions of all its elements. It is a unique St Petersburg interior of the first quarter of the nineteenth century, which has retained not only its original pictorial and sculptural decor, but also authentic furniture created after Rossi's designs. In some interiors the original decor has reached us only

The main staircase of the Russian Museum

The opening ceremony at the Alexander III Russian Museum on 7 March 1898. The artists, members of the Academy of Arts
Photograph

Medal struck to commemorate the establishment and opening of the Alexander III Russian Museum. 1898

СОБРАНІЕ УЗАКОНЕНІЙ И РАСПОРЯЖЕНІЙ ПРАВИТЕЛЬСТВА,
ИЗДАВАЕМОЕ ПРИ ПРАВИТЕЛЬСТВУЮЩЕМЪ СЕНАТѢ.

14 АПРѢЛЯ **№ 62.** **1895.**

СОДЕРЖАНІЕ:
Ст. 420. Объ учрежденіи особаго установленія подъ названіемъ «Русскаго Музея Императора Алек-
сандра III» и о предоставленіи для сей цѣли пріобрѣтеннаго въ казну Михайловскаго
Дворца со всѣми принадлежащими къ нему флигелями, службами и садомъ.

ИМЕННОЙ ВЫСОЧАЙШІЙ УКАЗЪ.

420. Объ учрежденіи особаго установленія подъ названіемъ «Русскаго Музея Императора Александра III» и о предоставленіи для сей цѣли пріобрѣтеннаго въ
казну Михайловскаго Дворца со всѣми принадлежащими къ нему флигелями,
службами и садомъ.

УКАЗЪ ПРАВИТЕЛЬСТВУЮЩЕМУ СЕНАТУ.

Незабвенный Родитель Нашъ, въ мудрой заботливости о развитіи
и процвѣтаніи отечественнаго искусства, предусматривалъ необходимость образо-
ванія въ С.-Петербургѣ обширнаго Музея, въ коемъ были бы сосредо-
точены выдающіяся произведенія русской живописи и ваянія. Таковому
высокополезному намѣренію почившаго Монарха не суждено было, однако
осуществиться при Его жизни.

Нынѣ, отвѣчая душевной потребности неотложно исполнить означен-
ную волю покойнаго Государя, признали Мы за благо учредить особое
установленіе подъ названіемъ «Русскаго Музея Императора Александра III»,
съ возложеніемъ главнаго завѣдыванія онымъ на одного изъ Членовъ
Императорскаго Дома по Нашему избранію, съ присвоеніемъ Ему званія
Управляющаго упомянутымъ Музеемъ.

Въ Музеѣ этомъ должна быть, прежде всего, отведена подобающая
важному ея значенію часть, посвященная памяти о жизни и Царствен-
ныхъ трудахъ Родителя Нашего. Съ тѣмъ вмѣстѣ, и впредь до составленія
этнографическихъ и историческихъ коллекцій, подлежитъ немедленному
устройству художественный отдѣлъ Музея, долженствующій обнимать собраніе картинъ и статуй лучшихъ русскихъ художниковъ, въ томъ числѣ
картины, пріобрѣтенныя для Музея въ Бозѣ почившимъ Императоромъ.

Дальнѣйшія подробности относительно устройства Музея и правила
о завѣдываніи онымъ имѣютъ быть выработаны согласно указаніямъ На-
шимъ и опредѣлены Положеніемъ о Русскомъ Музеѣ Императора Александра III.

Предусматривая, что для помѣщенія названнаго Музея въ полномъ его
составѣ потребуется зданіе значительныхъ размѣровъ, Повелѣваемъ пре-
доставить для сей цѣли пріобрѣтенный въ казну Михайловскій Дворецъ
со всѣми принадлежащими къ нему флигелями, службами и садомъ.

Да послужитъ учреждаемое хранилище живымъ воспоминаніемъ Цар-
ственныхъ заботъ и подвиговъ Того, Кто такъ горячо любилъ Родину и
посвятилъ Свою жизнь на служеніе ей.

На подлинномъ Собственною Его Императорскаго Величества рукою подписано:
Въ С.-Петербургѣ. «НИКОЛАЙ».
13 апрѣля 1895 года.

lic figures, politicians, scholars and writers gathered there. The musical classes created at the Mihailovsky Palace would later serve as the basis for the first Russian conservatory. It was in these classes that the great Tchaikovsky began his musical education. On 27 November 1865 he took the conductor's baton for the first time to perform his early *F-dur* overture in a room of the Mikhailovsky Palace — probably in the former Ballroom or the Large Dining-Room (Room 14, 15).

After 1873, the year of Yelena Pavlovna's death, the palace seemed to be gradually falling into a slumber for two decades. Life of its constant residents was concentrated in the more comfortable wings while the central part turned into a sort of memorial getting more and more decrepit.

On 13 April 1895 Emperor Nicholas II signed the Imperial Decree No 420 "On the foundation of the special establishment called 'The Russian Museum of Emperor Alexander III' and on allotting the Mikhailovsky Palace with all its wings, services and garden for this purpose." Three years later,

in fragments. These are the ceiling painting in the first passage drawing-room (Room 18, designed by Giovanni Scotti) executed in grisaille; the caryatids flanking the door opening (Room 16, sculptor Stepan Pimenov); the grisaille painting of the ceiling (Giovanni Scotti), the high-relief female heads (sculptor Stepan Pimenov) and the low-reliefs based on details of ancient Roman reliefs (sculptor Vasily Demuth-Malinovsky) in the drawing-room (Room 12) adjoining the White Hall. The other interiors were radically altered during numerous later attempts at reconstruction which were undertaken starting form the 1830s by various architects from Andrei Stakenschneider to Harald Bosse.

The palace's "pre-museum" period began in 1825 when those for whom it was intended, Grand Duke Mikhail Pavlovich and his wife Grand Duchess Yelena Pavlovna, née Frederika-Scharlotta-Maria, the Princess of Würtemburg, moved in. Life within the new walls was energetic and eventful. The first decades were the most brilliant and noisy time.

On the death of the grand duke in 1849 (the architect Carlo Rossi died in the same year) the striking luxury of high-society balls was succeeded by a more refined atmosphere of Yelena Pavlovna's artistic salon. Local and visiting celebrities, eminent pub-

on 7 March 1898, the doors of the Mikhailovsky Palace in St Petersburg flung open before visitors to the first state museum of national fine arts in Russia.

The idea to create the public Russian Museum, with the department of the visual arts occupying a prominent place in it, had been in the air long before the Emperor's decree. The specific feature of the situation was that this progressive idea was supported both by democratic society, usually in opposition to the activities of the government, and by Alexander III, who was thought to be, at least according to the official legend, a connoisseur and patron of national art. There is an important evidence of a man closely associated with the Emperor, who trained his artistic taste — the landscape painter Andrei Bogoliubov: "His Majesty himself suddenly told me: '...I often and seriously think of the necessity to create a museum of Russian art in St Petersburg. Moscow has the Tretyakov Gallery, though private yet fine, and, as I've heard, he bequeathed it to the city. And we have nothing here" (quoted from

A. V. Polovtsov, *A Tour around the Russian Museum of Emperor Alexander III in St Petersburg*, Moscow, 1900, p. 7).

But to meet the specific demands of museum life in the newly formed treasure-house of national art it was necessary not only to repair and restore the worn-out palace. The task of converting the building into a museum was much more complicated — to combine the luxury of the palace and comfort of its interiors with principally different exhibiting functions which were not inherent to Rossi's original project of the building. It was the architect Vasily Svinyin (1865–1939) who was entrusted to carry out this uneasy mission.

The young ambitious architect dreamed of creating the "Russian Louvre", but he had to listen to scathing comments of his contemporaries who were irritated by his allegedly too radical intrusion into the original concept. Admittedly, there were other, directly opposite opinions. The historical truth should be sought for, as usual, somewhere in the middle. At any rate it must be admitted that even after Svinyin's reconstruction the palace has remained a truly precious setting for no less valuable collections. Primarily, he left intact the general appearance of the palace, preserved some unique interiors and recreated in a number of cases the suite layout and the original design of the halls and rooms. The Great Academic Halls (Rooms 14 and 15) — the former Ballroom and Large Dining-Room — may be mentioned as examples of successful reconstruction. Having preserved the huge halls which used to accommodate up to a thousand guests during celebrations, Svinyin pierced windows in them and using up-to-date building technologies designed skylight illumination that befitted an art museum.

The original collection of painting, sculpture, graphic and applied art was not large

The central (southern) façade of the Mikhailovsky Palace

The garden (northern) façade of the Mikhailovsky Palace

B.-CH. MITOIRE
Portrait of the Architect Carlo Rossi. 1820s

GEORGE DAWE
Portrait of Grand Duke Mikhail Pavlovich
Early 1820s

ANSELME-FRANÇOIS LAGRÉNÉE
Portrait of Grand Duchess Yelena Pavlovna
Second half of the 1820s

The White Hall (Room 11)

View of the Cathedral
of the Resurrection
("Our Saviour-
on-the-Spilt-Blood")
and the Benois Block

The suite of rooms
on the first floor

and by the moment of the museum's inauguration numbered only some 1,500 works of art, with the collection of Christian antiquities amounting to 5,000 pieces. Today, when the museum boasts about 400,000 exhibits, these figures may seem more than modest, but for that early period its nucleus was quite sizeable.

There were not so many basic sources of acquisition. Practically the entire gallery of paintings by Russian artists, as well as a collection of sculpture, drawings and watercolours, were transferred from the Winter Palace and the Hermitage. A fairly large number of paintings, works of sculpture, watercolours and drawings was received

from the Museum of the Academy of Arts. The Academy also ceded its entire Museum of Christian Antiquities which contained very valuable pieces of ecclesiastical art. Nicholas II bought the collection of Prince Andrei Lobanov-Rostovsky from his successors and presented it to the Russian Museum. Princess Maria Tenisheva donated to the museum a significant part of her great collection of watercolours and drawings by Russian artists. And last, a sizeable contribution was Alexander III's private collection brought from the Alexander Palace at Tsarskoye Selo (the works preserved in the Anichkov Palace entered the museum later.) Throughout the first decade of its existence the museum has almost doubled its possessions. The addition to the museum's holdings of the famous collection of Russian and Greek icons by the well-known historian and art collector Nikolai Likhachev greatly enlarged its Department of Christian Antiquities. This acquisition made it possible to turn the department into the Depository of Works of Ancient Russian Icon-Painting and Church Antiquities, which became the largest state collection of icons in Russia. One more important addition was the collection of the "Pliushkin Museum", a donation made by an honourary hereditary citizen of Pskov, a first-guild merchant.

Nevertheless it is possible to speak about the museum's true establishment only after the appointment to the position of its Chief Curator of the artist Piotr Neradovsky. Within the two decades of his work in the museum he turned the disunited

The Large Academic Hall (Room 15). 1999

Academic Room XVII (now Room 15). 1898
Photograph

holdings into an integral, systematic and reasonably augmented collection.

The period from the late 1910s to the early 1920s saw a rapid growth of major state art collections and the Russian Museum was not an exclusion. The bulk of new additions were works of art arriving from the imperial and grand ducal residences — the Winter, Anichkov, Gatchina and Marble Palaces as well as from the Academy of Arts. The rearrangement of museum stocks undertaken during that period was made according to the specialization of each museum — the Hermitage, Russian Museum and the Tretyakov Gallery exchanged their exhibits. The State Museum Reserve which existed in 1921–28 and had many outstanding figures of Russian culture, professionals of museum work on its staff, played a considerable role in this process.

The course of history promoted the growth of the museum's holdings to such an extent that it could already represent any phases in the development of practically all kinds and genres of Russian fine arts. The further task faced by the museum was, while continuing to fill in gaps in the retrospective part of the collection, to pay more attention to the contemporary art process. In 1926 a collection of the recently closed State Institute of Artistic Culture, which contained works of the first quarter of the twentieth century, became the property of the museum. This acquisition formed the foundation of the world's largest collection of

The Large Academic Hall (Room 15). Before 1998

Room XXIII (now Room 16)
1898–1900s
Photograph

the Russian avant-garde that would be formed in the museum.

The arrangement of the original exhibition was not based on any scientific principles. The rooms of the museum produced a chaotic impression. The walls in many of them were hung with paintings of a very different artistic quality from top to bottom. The display was "decorated" with the "Memorial Section of Emperor Alexander III" arranged in the White Hall, its walls being lined with green plush. It was not until the second half of the 1920s that real efforts to create the museum display as an integral complex reflecting the development of national fine art were made under the guidance of Piotr Neradovsky. The exhibition, based on a chronological and, if possible, monographical principle, survives to the present day. The display was made with such loving care that Alexander Benois, on seeing it, exclaimed: "There is no national museum of this kind anywhere else in the world!"

The display area was gradually growing. The western block surviving from the original building and adjoining the left wing of the main edifice was completely freed to be used for flats of museum curators and for auxiliary services. In the 1930s, the so-called Benois Block overlooking the Griboyedov Canal was also given to the museum. This building was designed in 1910–12 by the architects Leonty Benois and Sergei Ovsiannikov to arrange exhibitions of various art societies and unions. Its foundation was laid on 27 June 1914, but the beginning of the war arrested the work and the construction was completed only in 1919. After the building had become the property of the museum, it began to house permanent displays of art of the late nineteenth and early twentieth centuries. Several rooms of the Benois Block were allotted for temporary exhibitions.

The early 1930s witnessed important changes in the structure of the museum. In 1934 the Ethnographical Department became an independent institution — the State Museum of the Ethnography of the Peoples of the Soviet Union. The "Memorial Department of Emperor Alexander III" had been earlier, in 1918, converted into a department of historical everyday life. Later it was partly transferred to the Hermitage, where it formed the core of the Department of Russian Culture.

But the nucleus of the collection, which made the Russian Museum a national treasure-house, was kept intact. Even the years of the Second World War did not bring any serious damage to it. The collection of the Russian Museum practically had no losses thanks only to the well-timed measures directed at the saving of its artistic treasures and to the heroic labour of a small number of the personnel who remained in the museum building during the war. The most valuable part of the collection was evacuated to the hinterland. The remaining works were safely hidden in the museum's basements. During the war more than forty shells exploded on the territory of the museum, over a hundred incendiary and eleven fougasse bombs were dropped on it. Four bombs, weighing 400 to 500 kilograms each, blew up right near the walls of the palace. As a result of these bomb attacks the foundation was damaged, the water supply system was destroyed and the window panes were broken. The Benois Block suffered the greatest damage — it was literally cleft by an explosion into two parts. But even during the war years the collection of the museum continued to grow. Numerous works found in deserted or destroyed houses were safely protected within the museum.

On 14 October 1945 a train with evacuated artistic treasures arrived in St Petersburg. And on 9 May 1946, the first anniversary of the victory over Nazism, the museum welcomed its first visitors in the ground-floor rooms. In the autumn of the same year the rooms of the first floor also became accessible. Later, on 8 November 1949, a display of the department of Soviet art opened in the restored Benois Block. Thus the restoration of the museum was finished. The construction in the post-war years of the passageway linking the main building with the Benois Block gave a unity and completeness to the overall display.

A decade ago such a brief historical survey of the museum's collections could be finished here. But the recent years, during which the Russian Museum celebrated its centenary, saw great changes in the life of the world-famous repository of Russian art. There is much in common between the situation which naturally led to the creation of the state-owned museum a century ago and present-day factors which resulted in the fast and decisive solution by the state authorities of numerous problems faced by the museum in connection with its immense and steadily growing holdings. It can be said without any reservation that the beginning of the twenty-first century marks for the Russian Museum a really new period associated both with the work to be done for bringing into use the newly received buildings and with the overcoming of those restrictions and dogmas of the past which have proved to be too rigid.

The recent years, during which the museum celebrated its centenary, saw great changes. Nowadays the museum occupies already four beautiful palaces in the central part of St Petersburg. All of them taken together build up a sort of panorama of the stylistic development of Russian architecture from the Baroque (the Stroganov Palace) and early and mature Classicism (Marble Palace and Engineers' Castle) to the Empire style (the Mikhailovsky Palace). The restored rooms of the palaces have already been used for new permanent displays; temporal exhibitions are also held there. At the same time further work on the restoration of unique monuments of Russian architecture is under way. The museum space will be expanded to the Mikhailovsky Garden which has been recently handed over to the Russian Museum. After restoration of the garden it will be decorated with bronze copies of original works by Russian sculptors of the eighteenth and nineteenth centuries kept in the museum.

Nowadays the museum carries out a complex programme of its development connected with a restoration and reconstruction of the original buildings and of those newly added to the museum. After the completion of the work a large-scale architectural and artistic complex named the "Russian Museum" will emerge in the centre of St Petersburg*.

View of the Academic Room (Room 15)

---

* The authors of the essay apologize for a lack of some works mentioned here and some alterations in the display.

Art of Ancient Russia

Icon: *The Archangel Gabriel (The Angel with the Golden Hair)*
12th century
Tempera on panel
49 x 38.8 cm*

———————
*All dimensions are given in centimetres

The State Russian Museum, along with the Tretyakov Gallery and the Historical Museum in Moscow, possesses one of the largest and most representative collections of works of medieval Russian art. It amounts to more than five thousand icons and about 500,000 pieces of jewellery, church utensils and devotional objects.

The first works of early Russian art began to enter the collection in 1898 from the Academy of Arts — its Museum of Christian Antiquities, established in 1858, had collections of wooden sculpture and works of applied art (mostly church articles), as well as more than 1,500 icons.

Later the holdings of the Russian Museum were enriched with works transferred from monasteries and churches, as well as with items received from private collections which had grown in number and size towards the end of the nineteenth century. The Church itself, concerned with the preservation of its objects having lasting artistic value, not infrequently handed them over to the museum where they would be kept in special conditions, far from vicissitudes of life and detrimental effects of the elements. Emperor Nicholas II, taking care of the first state-owned

Ear-rings decorated with birds. First half of the 12th century
Kiev
Silver, engraved and niellated
8 x 7.4 x 1.9; 8.2 x 7.5 x 2

Riasny (necklace). First half of the 12th century
Kiev
Gold, cloisonné enamel.
Diameter of plaques: 2.7

Icon: *The Virgin Eleusa of Belozerye.* First half of the 13th century
Tempera on panel. 155 x 100

Icon: *SS John the Climacus, George and Blase.* Second half of the 13th century Novgorod Tempera on panel. 109 x 67.4

Icon: *St Nicholas* Mid-13th century Novgorod Tempera on panel. 67.5 x 52.8

Icon: *The Miracle of St George.* 15th century Novgorod Tempera on panel. 58 x 41.5

museum of national art, used to acquire notable icons and present them to the museum, in most cases anonymously.

By 1914 the museum had accumulated a sizeable collection of early Russian art, the largest in the country, and this resulted in the establishment of the special section named "The Emperor Nicholas II Depository of Works of Ancient Russian Icon-Painting and Church Antiquities".

A large number of most remarkable present-day exhibits have occupied the pride of place in the museum already in that period.

The revolution of 1917 not only annihilated most of believers faithful to the Church, but affected the preservation of

ecclesiastical art too. Thousands of unique artifacts were saved from destruction and plundering only thanks to the enthusiasm of the museum personnel. The Second World War and its consequences demanded new efforts for the preservation of the ancient heritage. In the 1950s and 1960s the Russian Museum organized special expeditions to distant regions which yielded many valuable works dating from the fourteenth to nineteenth centuries. They were rescued from damp, neglected churches or were acquired from the homes of local people.

The collection of early Russian art which is now the pride of Russian culture has been mainly formed by the 1960s. The permanent displays is devoted to old Russian icons; the rooms devoted to decorative arts are to be opened after reconstruction. The icons are arranged in a chronological sequence in four first-floor rooms of the Mikhailovsky Palace (Nos 1–4). A very special atmosphere, reminding of the initial, purely spiritual designation of the works shown there, reigns in these rooms.

As Father Pavel Florensky, an outstanding Russian theologian, wrote at the beginning of the twentieth century, "the faces of saints seem dark for a darkened soul and seem to be arrested in awful immobility for the paralyzed one. <...> But pure eyes still see the saints' faces in their brilliance... For the cleansed heart they are no less warm than before; and as in the olden times they appeal to those who have ears to hear."

The most ancient icon in the collection of the Russian Museum is ***Archangel***

Gabriel (The Angel with the Golden Hair) ******* (12th century). Although small in size, the icon produces a monumental impression. The angel's head with the huge, wide-opened, almond-shaped eyes dominates the icon. The outlines of his face are rendered in simple and powerful manner. The rich hair skirting the face and falling down the shoulders is somewhat decorative. We do not know who painted the icon and how it found its way to one of Russian churches. But the golden thread — a symbol of the grandeur and immortality of the Gods of Olympus — suggest the Hellenistic traditions inherited by Byzantium during the Middle Ages.

Peeping into the icons and thinking about their striking blend of soft, almost lyrical and humane treatment, lofty spirituality and austere asceticism, one might surmise that the festive appearance of icons

Icon: *SS Boris and Gleb*
Mid-14th century. Moscow
Tempera on panel. 162 x 104

Icon: *The Descent into Hell*
Late 14th century. Pskov
Tempera on panel. 82 x 66

Icon: *Our Saviour of the Fiery Eye*
Late 14th – early 15th century. Moscow
Tempera on panel. 107.2 x 78.3

Pall: *Agnus Dei*. 15th century
Novgorod
Taffeta, silk, golden and silver thread. 42 x 41

*The works which are reproduced in this art book are indicated in the text in bold-face. The names of the artists whose works are reproduced are also accentuated.

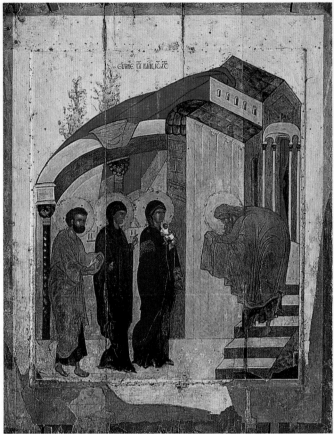

Icon: *The Presentation in the Temple*
The Raising of Lazarus
The Holy Trinity
St John the Divine on Patmos Island. First half of the 15th century
Novgorod
Tempera on panel. 103 x 76.5

Icon: *The Presentation in the Temple.* Ca 1408
Moscow
Tempera on panel. 124.5 x 92

DIONYSIUS
AND HIS WORKSHOP
Icon: *The Incredulity of St Thomas.* Ca 1500
Tempera on panel. 85 x 54

played an important role in the choice of the Orthodox faith made in Constantinople by the messengers of Russia, eager to acquire its religion, in the tenth century.

The national character of icons became increasingly prominent over the centuries — the evolution can be noticed in the gradual introduction of the typically Russian facial features, in the favourable colour scheme (not infrequently determined by the locally available set of mineral pigments), and in compositional, rhythmic and ornamental peculiarities of local Russian schools of icon-painting.

A distinctive feature of the collection of the Russian Museum is a large number of icons which have originated from the Russian North. It is quite natural — Novgorod, Pskov, Vologda, Belozersk and Archangel are not very distant from St Petersburg.

The icon of **The Virgin Eleusa of Belozerye** (first half of the 13th century) was discovered in the Cathedral of the Transfiguration at Belozersk. However, originally it had not been intended for it since the cathedral was built only in the eighteenth century. This icon is the earliest and rarest example of the iconographical type known as the Virgin Eleusa (the Child Christ is shown embracing His Mother and His face is touching Her cheek) and evolved in Byzantium not later than the eleventh century. The images of the Prophets, Archangels and the Holy Women, which go back to the still earlier tradition, are portrayed in its margins. But all of them are connected with the central image — Jeremiah, Isaiah and St John the Precursor foretold the coming of the Messiah and King David is the primogenitor of the kin to which St Mary belonged.

The icon **St Boris and St Gleb** (mid-14th century, Moscow) is perhaps one the most impressive works of medieval art to have survived. The outstanding artistic merits of the icon became especially apparent after its cleaning carried out by restorers at the Russian Museum in the late 1980s. The deep blue colour of the shroud and the gold ornament on the fabric have regained their former intensity lending to the icon a festive and solemn mood. St Boris and St Gleb were brothers, sons of Prince Vladimir, who initiated the baptism of Russia. On the latter's death an internecine feud began in which the brothers were killed. Revered as holy defenders, St Boris and St Gleb were quite popular in Russia. Historical records were written about the saint brothers starting from the eleventh century, churches were consecrated to them and their conventional portraits were

painted. The icon in the Russian Museum portrays St Boris and St Gleb with their indispensable attributes — the cross symbolizing a martyr's death and the sword typifying both power and protection.

Represented in the Russian Museum are all schools of icon-painting which existed in Russia in the Middle Ages, a period when each city had the artistic traditions of its own. The museum's collection of icons allows one to trace the differences characteristic of the exhibits created by icon-painters in Novgorod, Pskov, Vologda and Moscow as well as in other artistic centres.

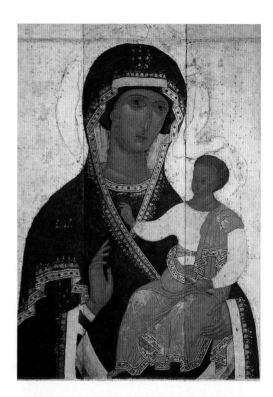

The luxurious red and golden icons from the Novgorod area prevail in the collection of the Russian Museum. The icon *The Battle of the Novgorodians and the Suzdalians* (early 14th century) stands out among them not only for its colour range and compositional solution. This unique work is connected with the real events and is in fact the first history painting in Russia. Next to Novgorod icons hang examples of the Pskov School of icon-painting which are more austere in colour and composition and share more features with folk art in their chromatic and plastic idiom.

The Resurrection – The Descent into the Limbo (late 14th century) is a Pskov icon. It shows the resurrected Christ who, standing over the black abyss of Hell, guides Kings David and Solomon, the Old Testament Prophets and Forefathers out of it. This subject was widespread in Russian icons.

It is in this example that the subject of the Harrowing of Hell has acquired the most dramatic colouring. The contrasts of black, red and golden, the abrupt movements and the angular plasticity of the figures enhance the scene's tension. But the highlights applied upon the faces and clothes

Icon: *The Miracle of the Icon of Our Lady of the Sign (The Battle of the Novgorodians and the Suzdalians)*
Early 16th century
Novgorod
Tempera on panel. 133 x 90

DIONYSIUS
AND HIS WORKSHOP
Icon: *The Virgin Hodegetria.* 1502–03
Tempera on panel
141.2 x 105.7

Altar-cloth:
St Irene the Martyr. Late 16th – early 17th century
Moscow. Workshop
of Irina Godunova
Damask, silk, golden
and silver thread. 70 x 66

ANDREI RUBLEV
1360/70 – *ca* 1430
Icon: *The Apostle Peter*
The Apostle Paul. Ca 1408
From the Deesis tier of the
Church of the Assumption
of the Virgin in Vladimir
Tempera on panel. 312 x 105;
311 x 104

Icon: *The Old Testament*
Trinity. Mid-16th century
Novgorod
Tempera on panel. 148.9 x 113.5

GREEK CRAFTSMEN
Altar cross. 1576
Silver, forged, engraved and
gilded, coloured enamels
44.4 x 22.5 x 2

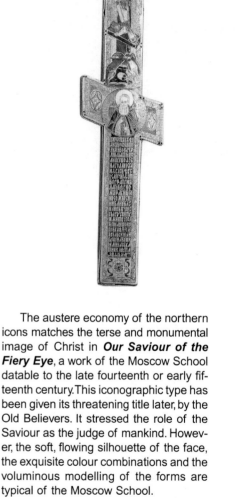

The Miracle of St George
First half of the 16th century
Tempera on panel; carving
29 x 22.4 x 1.8

and emphasizing the volumes create a festive impression. The golden auxiliary tone on the garments' details enriches the simple and concise colour scheme of the icon.

The austere economy of the northern icons matches the terse and monumental image of Christ in **Our Saviour of the Fiery Eye**, a work of the Moscow School datable to the late fourteenth or early fifteenth century. This iconographic type has been given its threatening title later, by the Old Believers. It stressed the role of the Saviour as the judge of mankind. However, the soft, flowing silhouette of the face, the exquisite colour combinations and the voluminous modelling of the forms are typical of the Moscow School.

Of great value in the collection of the Russian Museum are works by Andrei Rublev, the celebrated icon-painter active in Moscow. The icon **The Apostle Paul** and its companion, **The Apostle Peter** (both 1408), come from the Deesis Tier of the Cathedral of the Dormition in Vladimir. Working on these icons, Andrei Rublev took into account that the icons were intended for a high tier of the iconostasis. This accounts for a lack of details in the representations and its clear-cut silhouettes. The massive figures

of St Peter and St Paul are nearly completely concealed by the folds of their garments.

The colouristic treatment based on the blend of the greenish-blue colour with a yellow background (originally it was golden) endows the image with a quiet and solemn atmosphere.

The museum owns several icons by Dionysius and his workshop. ***The Incredulity of St Thomas*** (*ca* 1500) is a subject usually represented in the festive tier of the Orthodox iconostasis. The icon from the Pavlo-Obnorsky Monastery in Vologda Region features a moment when St Thomas, one of Christ's disciples, wishing to ascertain the true resurrection of the Teacher, touched His wound. His incredulity has disappeared and he is looking at Christ with veneration, fear and admiration. The hand of St Thomas and his entire bowed figure compositionally continue the line of Christ's hand directed at His wound. Christ is shown above all others, mercifully and understandingly forgiving the incredulity.

The Virgin Hodegetria (1502–03) comes from the Cathedral of the Nativity of the Virgin in the St Therapont Monastery (it was part of the local tier of icons). The thin, transparent painting of the faces, the blue shimmering of the garments, and the gold of the decorative patterns and ornaments create a vivid colouristic effect. The clear-cut outline of the figures, the austere majesty of their postures and gestures endow the representation with a feeling

SIMON USHAKOV
Icon: *The Holy Trinity*. 1671
Tempera on panel. 123 x 89.2

NIKIFOR SAVIN
Icon: *The Miracle of St George*. First half
of the 17th century. Tempera on panel. 35.2 x 29.8

***Archbishop John of Novgorod*.** 1559
The image taken off the cover of the shrine
Tempera on carved wood. 192 x 56 x 12

Altar Gospels. 1681. Moscow
Gold, silver, gems, glass, forged, cast, chased, carved,
gilded, niellated and enamelled. 44 x 26.5 x 13

of grandeur and significance. The hand of Christ lying on the blue trian-
gle of the Virgin's cloak edged with gold is the focus of the entire icon.

An acquaintance with Western originals (e.g. the Piscator Bible), trace-
able in many works of various schools during the seventeenth century,
is especially distinct in Yaroslavl icons. A tendency towards verisimilitude,
a departure from the traditional red-yellow colour were characteristic of
Simon Ushakov, an icon-painter of the transitional period. He first worked
at the Moscow Armoury as a silversmith and later as an icon-painter.
Ushakov was a universal artist. He created miniatures for church books,
worked as an engraver, wrote treatises on icon-painting, painted *parsu-
nas* (portraits combining the features of icons and secular paintings) and,
of course, created icons. Works by Simon Ushakov are remarkable for
their modelling of shapes and attempts to introduce direct perspective,
borrowed from Western European artists, into traditional iconic imagery.

The icon in Russia, with all its seeming rigidity and canonical patterns, gradually changed its forms and stylistic devices. The mounts of
icons were also important. Sometimes a mount would cover the larger
part of the representation lending the icon a more decorative and ornate
appearance. The mounts, usually made by skilled craftsmen, are now preserved as valuable works of art together with icons or separately from
them. The emergence of icon mounts marks the penetration of secular
elements into church culture. The sixteenth and especially the seventeenth century saw a distinct tendency to render volume, to attain verisimilitude and to make emphasis on decorative qualities.

Russian Art
of the 18th Century

JOHANN TANNAUER
(1680–1737/3?)
*Peter the Great during
the Battle of Poltava*
1724/5?
Oil on canvas. 76 x 63.5
The Marble Palace

Touring the rooms of eighteenth-century art (Nos 5–10, 12), you will follow the path traversed by the country in this century — from the barbarously naive noisy "assemblies" and "the All-joking, All-drinking Council of Fools and Jesters" to the European Enlightenment, from the reign of Peter I to that of Catherine the Great. In art it was the path from the turbulence and dynamism of the Baroque to the austere regularity of Classicism.

The end of the seventeenth and especially the beginning of the eighteenth century, the reign of Peter the Great, was the age of radical reforms which stirred up Russia, entangled in its long caftans, to action. Peter the Great laid the basis for the education of Russia's own national artists, architects and sculptors, and he could even enjoy the first

UNKNOWN ARTIST
**Portrait of Yakov
Turgenev.** Before 1695
Oil on canvas. 105 x 97.5

successive results. A group of young talents were given an opportunity to study in Europe. Among Peter's pensioners sent to Italy was **Ivan Nikitin** (*ca* 1680 – not earlier than 1742). One of his best works is **Portrait of a Hetman** (1720s). The sitter's name is unknown but whoever the person portrayed might be, the artist created an image remarkable for its power and expressiveness. The painting has something in common with canvases by Titian and Rembrandt seen by Nikitin in Italy. Worthy of mention among Nikitin's other notable works in the museum is *Peter the Great on His Deathbed* (1725),

IVAN NIKITIN
Ca 1680 – after 1742
Portrait of a Hetman. 1720s
Oil on canvas. 70 x 60

ROMAN NIKITIN
Not earlier than 1680 – 1753
Portrait of Maria Stroganova
Between 1721 and 1724
Oil on canvas. 111 x 90

his last tribute to the Emperor who undoubtedly valued Nikitin more highly than other artists. Another painter promoted by Peter the Great was **Andrei Matveyev** (1701/04–1739) who also trained abroad (in Holland) during Peter's reign and created skilful paintings in a European manner, such as *The Artist's Self-Portrait with His Wife* (1729?).

The early eighteenth century saw the emergence of a new system of values and thinking which was introduced, sometimes forcefully, instead of the universally applied religious ideology. A large-scale programme of constructing secular masonry buildings along with churches and cathedrals was under way. Many architects, sculptors and painters were invited from Germany, Holland, France, Italy and other European countries. Together with Russian craftsmen they built palaces and mansions which were then embellished with portraits, landscapes and still lifes. At the beginning of the eighteenth century an inevitable process of the influence

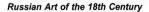

ANDREI MATVEYEV
Between 1701 and 1704–39
**The Artist's Self-Portrait
with His Wife.** 1729 (?)
Oil on canvas. 75.5 x 90.5

ÀLEXEI BELSKY. 1729(?)–1796
Flowers, Fruit and Parrot
1754. Panel
Oil on canvas. 99 x 208

LOUIS CARAVAQUE. 1684–1754
**Portrait of Tsarevnas
Anna Petrovna and
Elizabeth Petrovna.** 1717
Oil on canvas. 78 x 97

Perfume vase
Mid-18th century
The Imperial Porcelain
Factory, St Petersburg
Porcelain, carved, modelled,
painted in colours over a glaze
and gilded. Height 33.8

of European artistic experience on Russian culture took place.

The collection of the Russian Museum contains a huge section of the so-called "Rossica" — paintings, sculptures, engravings and drawings produced by foreign artists in Russia during the eighteenth and nineteenth centuries. Part of these works make up the display "Foreign Artists of the 18th and 19th Centuries Active in Russia" arranged in the Marble Palace recently. Worthy of special note among them is the painting ***Peter the Great during the Battle of Poltava*** (1724/5?) by **Johann Gottfried Tannauer** (1680–1737/3?) — an allegorical portrait based on the subject of Peter's historical victory at Poltava in 1709. The gem of the exhibition in the Mikhailovsky Castle is the bronze group ***Empress Anna Ioannovna with a Moorish Boy*** (1741),

ANTON LOSENKO. 1737–1773
Vladimir and Rogneda. 1770
Oil on canvas. 211.5 x 177.5

ALEXEI ZUBOV. 1682–1751
View of St Petersburg. 1727
Etching, burin. 24.2 x 33.7

IVAN VISHNIAKOV. 1699–1761
Portrait of Sarah Eleanor Fermore. *Ca* 1750
Oil on canvas. 138 x 114.5

CARLO BARTOLOMEO RASTRELLI. 1675–1744
Empress Anna Ioannovna with a Moorish Boy. 1741
Bronze. 223 x 228 x 228

FIODOR ROKOTOV. 1730s–1808
Portrait of Countess Elizabeth Santi. 1785
Oil on canvas. 72.5 x 56

IVAN ARGUNOV. 1727–1802
**Portrait of Princess
Yekaterina Lobanova-Rostovskaya.** 1754
Oil on canvas. 81.5 x 62.5

a work by **Carlo Bartolommeo Rastrelli** (1675–1744), father of the great designer of the Winter Palace. The clear-cut forms of the powerful figure encased in a formal dress are rendered by the sculptor carefully and with a naturalness verging on an illusory effect.

The process of inculcating the European standards into Russian culture vigorously supported by Peter the Great and his successors was not as fast and simple as it might seem. The nearly seven centuries of the dominance of icon-painting had a deep imprint on the artistic memory of Russia. **The Portrait of Sarah Eleanor Fermore** (*ca* 1750) testifies to the undoubted talent and superb skill of its painter, **Ivan Vishniakov** (1699–1761). This portrait has an apparent affinity to European examples, but its flat treatment of space and economy of colour are vestiges of icon-painting.

A little later portraiture became as popular in Russia as elsewhere throughout Europe. Both small intimate portraits and huge formal likenesses of members of the nobility from that period make up an interesting and important part of the collection of the Russian Museum. With all

their European orientation and outward effects, paintings by some artists, such as *Portrait of Princess Yekaterina Lobanova-Rostovskaya* (1754) by **Ivan Argunov** (1727–1802), still echo the medieval traditions. The complete elimination of their traces was probably connected with the foundation in St Petersburg of Russia's own Academy of Arts in the middle of the 1760s.

The Russian Museum owns a brilliant collection of examples of academic art from its burgeoning to the present day. The reasons for such fullness were the proximity of the Acad-

emy to the museum and, naturally, the prestige of the imperial depository which had always attracted both artists and art collectors. The Russian Museum preserves and displays paintings by the first professors of the Academy which are important as early examples of Russian secular painting: *Zeus and Thetis* (1769), *Vladimir and Rogneda* (1770) and other works by **Anton Losenko** (1737–1773); *Mercury and Argus* (1776) and *Venus and Adonis* (1782) by **Piotr Sokolov**. Losenko's picture *Vladimir and Rogneda* played a special role in the formation of the historical genre as a distinct kind of painting in Russia. Losenko took an episode from national history for this canvas. The action is set in the tenth century when the baptism of Old Russia by Prince Vladimir took place. The painting deals with an episode when the prince wished to marry Rogneda, a daughter of the Polovtian king, and despite her resistance attained his goal by cunning and power.

History painting was considered the most important specialty on the list of priorities at the St Petersburg Academy of Arts (as in all European Academies). Nevertheless, future landscape painters, artists of everyday scenes, portraitists, engravers, architects and sculptors were also trained.

The late eighteenth and early nineteenth centuries saw the flowering of portraiture in Russia. The dominant figure in the art of the 1770s and 1780s was **Fiodor Rokotov** (1730s–1808), one of the most subtle and elegant portrait painters of the period. The Russian Museum owns about forty of his works. *Portrait of Elizabeth Santi* (1785) ranks with the best of them. As is usual with Rokotov's portraits, the image is put

FIODOR ALEXEYEV
1753/4–1824
**View of the Peter and
Paul Fortress and Palace
Embankment.** 1799
Oil on canvas. 17.5 x 109

Toilet glass
Late 18th – early 19th century
Kholmogory, Archangel
Province
Carved bone, foil and glass
81 x 54 x 19

FEDOT SHUBIN. 1740–1805
**Catherine the Great
as a Legislatress.** 1789
Marble. 198 x 114 x 188

ANTON LOSENKO. 1737–1773
Abraham's Sacrifice. 1765
Oil on canvas. 202 x 157

FIODOR MATVEYEV. 1758–1826
Waterfall at Tivoli
Black chalk on grey paper. 69.1 x 51.3

PIOTR SOKOLOV. 1753–1791
Venus and Adonis. 1782
Oil on canvas. 252 x 165

FEDOT SHUBIN. 1740–1805
Portrait of Paul I. 1800
Marble. 80 x 53 x 33

into an oval. The artist uses the subtlest glazes to convey the texture, the facial features and the transparent softness of the gauze used to trim the lady's dress.

Sculptural portraits by **Fedot Shubin** (1740–1805), Rokotov's contemporary, are remarkable not so much for their physical verisimilitude as for their delineation of the characters. Shubin's **bust of Paul I** (1800) produces an unusual effect thanks to an abrupt turn of the head with regard to the body. Walking around the sculpture the visitor can see how the sitter's expression is gradually changing.

Dmitry Levitsky (1735–1822) is the most brilliant Russian portrait painter of the age of Classicism. His series of seven portraits featuring the students of the Smolny Institute for noble girls, the future ladies-in-waiting to the Empress, was commissioned from Levitsky

Statuettes: *The Kurilian,*
The Estland Woman,
The Ukrainian Cossack
From the series
The Peoples of Russia
1780s–1790s.
After models by
Jean-Dominique Rachette
The Imperial Porcelain
Factory, St Petersburg.
Porcelain, painted in colours
over a glaze and gilded
Height 20.8; 20.8; 20.6

DMITRY LEVITSKY. 1735–1822
Portrait of
the Aide-de-Camp
Alexander Lanskoi. 1782
Oil on canvas. 151 x 117

DMITRY LEVITSKY. 1735–1822
Portrait of Yekaterina
Khrushchova
and Yekaterina
Khovanskaya. 1773
Oil on canvas. 164 x 129

by Catherine the Great and illustrates the Age of Enlightenment. The Smolny Institute was founded in St Petersburg as a privileged educational establishment in 1764. Daughters of members of the nobility were trained there for secular life and for court service. The girls developed talents of pleasance — they were taught to sing, dance, play musical instruments, speak good French and German. Various performances were staged at the Institute with the girls' participation. In his *Portrait of Yekaterina Khrushchova and Yekaterina Khovanskaya* (1773) Levitsky showed each of his models in the guise that seemed more suitable to her. Khrushcheva, who was older, played the part of a shepherd. Khovanskaya was portrayed as the shepherd's younger girl-friend. The richly textured white and pink silk of the dress and the grey moiré of the caftan are perfectly rendered. The composition of the double portrait enclosed in an oval, lends a sense of harmony, calm and elevation of spirit to the entire scene.

Portrait of Alexander Lanskoi (1782), a lover of Catherine the Great, who ascended from the poor nobility to the rank of General-Aide-de-Camp is an excellent example

VLADIMIR BOROVIKOVSKY
1757–1825
Portrait of Yekaterina Arsenyeva. Second half of the1790s
Oil on canvas. 71.5 x 56.5

VLADIMIR BOROVIKOVSKY
1757–1825
Portrait of Major-General Fiodor Borovsky. 1799
Oil on canvas. 80.5 x 62.5

of a representative portrait endowed with symbols and allegories. Lanskoi's painted likeness is displayed next to a sculptural portrait of his patroness Catherine the Great.

Towards the end of the eighteenth century an increasingly large emphasis began to be laid on man's closeness to nature, on everything natural. Large-scale formal portraits were still produced in which the sitter was encircled with objects epitomizing his or her private life and social activity. But there were few portraits of this kind in the work of **Vladimir Borovikovsky** (1757–1825). The majority of his portraits (there are more than thirty of them in the Russian Museum) fully conform to the aesthetic principles of Sentimentalism. Borovikovsky usually captures his sitters in sensitive or sensuous states depicting them in a lightened colour scheme, as exemplified by his *Portrait of Yekaterina Arsenyeva* (second half of the 1790s). The young girl is merry, careless and coquettish; she wears a white dress reminiscent of an ancient chiton in its cut and a gold-coloured straw "shepherdess's" hat. Her simple and elegant clothes reflect the fashion of those days.

The expression of national features was a leitmotif of Russian artistic culture throughout the eighteenth century. *Testing the Strength of Yan Usmar* (1796/97), a painting by **Grigory Uriumov** (1764–1823), is a fine example of classical art showing that its prin-

GRIGORY UGRIUMOV
1764–1823
*Testing the Strength
of Yan Usmar.* 1796/97
Oil on canvas. 283 x 404

MIKHAIL IVANOV. 1728–1823
*Prince Potemkin-
Tavrichesky with a Cavalry
Detachment on the Neva
Embankment.* 1798
Watercolour on paper. 59.5 x 45.8

IVAN MARTOS. 1754–1835
*Tombstone of Princess
Yelena Kurakina.* 1792
Plaster of Paris. 104 x 164 x 80

ciples were thoroughly mastered by the Russian artist. The subject of the painting is based on a legend about Yan Usmar, a young man who demonstrated his physical force to Prince Vladimir by fighting an enraged bull.

Thus, you have walked around the rooms which illustrate a very interesting period in the development of the fine arts in Russia. Discarding the canons and precepts of icon-painting in the early eighteenth century, the artists of this period turned to the traditions of Classical Antiquity — the no less rigid system of artistic laws born in the even more distant times — towards the end of the century.

Russian Art
of the 19th Century

SYLVESTER SHCHEDRIN
1791–1830
Terrace on the Seashore:
Capuccini near
Sorrento. 1827
Oil on canvas. 47.5 x 60

From the rooms featuring works by artists active mainly in the eighteenth century visitors proceed to the White Hall. Its interior typifies the Russian Empire style predominant during a phase of transition from Classicism to Romanticism at the end of the 1810s and the beginning of the 1820s. From the White Hall begins the display of Russian art dating from the first half of the nineteenth century (Rooms 13 to 17).

During the first half of the nineteenth century Russia was involved in the events of world significance, notably the war against Napoleon's Army which began around the middle of the 1800s and ended in 1814 by the triumphal entry of the Russian troops into Paris. All strata of society were in some way engaged in the war. Russian people shared sorrows after disasters and joys after victories and this erased social barriers between them.

OREST KIPRENSKY. 1782–1836
Portrait of the Artist's
Father Adam Schwalbe
1804
Oil on panel. 78.2 x 64.1

OREST KIPRENSKY. 1782–1836
Portrait of Yekaterina
Avdulina. 1822(3?)
Oil on canvas. 81 x 64.3

The war had a great impact on the views of the whole generation. Art of the first decades of the nineteenth century is often called the age of Pushkin. In the thirties the ideal heroes and sentimental dreamers were ousted by the realistic man whose value was determined by his wit, his talents and the daring of his accomplishments rather than by the smartness of his figure and facial features. A search for an idyllic harmony lost its predominance. The Romantic hero showed his readiness to engage in a single combat or even in an unequal, sometimes fatal fight. Unlike classical ancient characters,

ANDREI IVANOV. 1776–1848
The Feat of a Kievan Youth during the Siege of Kiev by the Pechenegs in 968. *Ca* 1810
Oil on canvas. 204 x 177.5

OREST KIPRENSKY. 1782–1836
Portrait of M. Lanskoi. 1822(3?)
Black chalk on paper. 25.4 x 20

OREST KIPRENSKY. 1782–1836
Portrait of Retired Major-General Karl Albrecht. 1827
Oil on canvas. 196.5 x 138.5

OREST KIPRENSKY. 1782–1836
Portrait of Life-Guards Colonel Yevgraf Davydov. 1809
Oil on canvas. 162 x 116

he sacrifices his life not for the sake of abstract social ideals alone, but for the sake of self-assertion too, casting by his demonstrative death a challenge to the injustice of fate, indifference of society or unrequited love.

Romanticism in Russia, similarly to Europe, was not a unified or only movement. On coming during your tour of the museum to the room where art of the middle and second half of the nineteenth century is displayed, you can trace how a new, different stylistic trend is burgeoning and gaining strength. Romanticism developed along two different lines, which had revealed themselves earlier in Russian art: the poetic depiction of ordinary, "non-heroic" people, quiet everyday life, customary national landscapes, on the one side, and strong emphasis on the tragic dissonance between man and the circumstances of his life, between man and society or the state.

KARL BRIULLOV. 1799–1852
Portrait of the Shishmarev Sisters. 1839
Oil on canvas. 281 x 213

KARL BRIULLOV. 1799–1852
Vladimir Kornilov on Board the Brig "Themistocles". 1835
Watercolour and black chalk on paper. 40.4 x 28.9

KARL BRIULLOV. 1799–1852
Portrait of K. and M. Naryshkin. 1827
Watercolour on paper. 44.1 x 35.4

**Vase with a representation of Palace Square
in St Petersburg.** Early 1830s
Painted decoration after an engraving by L. Tumling
The Batenin Factory, St Petersburg
Porcelain, painted in colours over a glaze, gilded and cirrated
43 x 22 x 20

KARL BRIULLOV. 1799–1852
**The Last Day
of Pompeii.** 1833
Oil on canvas. 456.5 x 651

The holdings of the Russian Museum provide a unique possibility to show the entire gamut of art trends and artistic quests which existed in the first half of the nineteenth century. The exhibits dated to this period are one of the richest parts of the collection — before the revolution of 1917 St Petersburg was the capital of the Empire and the best works were naturally brought to the first national art museum. Many works by artists of the first half of the nineteenth century entered the Russian Museum from the Academy of Arts and from palaces and mansions left by their owners.

Portrait of the Artist's Father (1804) by **Orest Kiprensky** (1782–1836) is simple and terse. The dark background and clothes serve to frame and emphasize the powerfully painted face with fiery eyes. An imitation of Rembrandt's restless, dramatic images and a deliberately sharp treatment of strong and energetic characters to evoke a response of the viewer — these are the characteristic features of Kiprensky's work created long before his first travel to Italy in 1816, where the Russian

Tray with a view of the estate of Arkhangelskoye near Moscow. 1831
The Yusupov Factory,
Village of Arkhangelskoye,
Moscow Province
Porcelain, painted in colours
over a glaze and gilded. 31 x 23

Statuettes: *Smart Man, Smart Woman.* 1830s.
The Safronov Factory,
Moscow Province
Porcelain, painted in colours
over a glaze. Height 17.5

Furniture set. First
quarter of the 19th century
After sketches by
Carlo Rossi
Wood, carved and gilded

artist could familiarize himself with examples of the Romantic movement.

In 1809 Orest Kiprensky painted his ***Portrait of Yevgraf Davydov*** which became a symbol of early Russian Romanticism. The image of Davydov combining dreaminess and pride, ease and theatricality, conveys the worldview and manner of conduct quite popular in Russian society during the Napoleonic campaign.

In 1812–15 Orest Kiprensky painted portraits of many **participants in the war against Napoleon**. As a rule these were rapid drawings in black chalk, executed within several hours. Servicemen were shown in uniforms, with insignia. But Kiprensky's attention was invariably focused on the sitter's face as an expression of his emotional state. Man's inner world became for Kiprensky and other contemporary painters the primary aim of artistic observation.

After his travel to Italy and France Kiprensky painted ***Portrait of Yekaterina Avdulina*** (1822–23), now in the Russian

Museum. Art scholars sometimes compare this canvas, one of the best creations in Russian art of the first half of the nineteenth century, with works by Ingres. Indeed, Kiprensky's love for graphically clear-cut outlines suggests some affinity with the famous artist. However, the Russian master is more lyrical and soft in the rendering of the character and mood of his sitter.

In 1828, after staying in Russia for five years (1823–28), Kiprensky left for Italy again. He was not destined to return to his native country. But when he was going to come back to St Petersburg, he dispatched there from Rome his personal belongings, including his pictures. Some of them are now in the Russian Museum and illustrate an evolution in Kiprensky's creative career.

The Romantic perception of the world which became predominant in the artistic circles of Russia in the early nineteenth century exerted a strong influence on Russian landscape painting and graphic art.

FIODOR BRUNI. 1799–1875
**The Death of Camilla,
Sister of the Horatii.** 1824
Oil on canvas. 350 x 526.5

FIODOR BRUNI. 1799–1875
The Brazen Serpent. 1841
Oil on canvas. 565 x 852

ALEXEI VENETSIANOV
1780–1847
Threshing-Barn. 1821(2?)
Oil on canvas. 66.5 x 80.5

GRIGORY SOROKA
1823–1864
**View of the Mansion
at Ostrovki, Nikolai
Miliukov's Manor.** 1844
Oil on canvas. 54 x 65

FIODOR TOLSTOI. 1783–1873
The People's Volunteer Corps: The Year 1812
1816. Medallion
Wax on slate. Diameter 16

Vase: Volcano and Thetis
From the Ministry Service
1827
The Imperial Porcelain Factory, St Petersburg
Porcelain, painted in colours over a glaze and gilded
60.2 x 32.2

BORIS ORLOVSKY. 1797–1837
Fawn and Bacchante. 1837
Marble. 183 x 90 x 54

Sylvester Shchedrin (1791–1830), active in Italy near the Posilippo School, created inspired scenes of Rome, Naples, Sorrento and other notable places.

Changing its appearance and combining with other trends and movements, Romanticism remained popular in Russia for quite a long time. While early Romantic portraits were marked by lyricism and an intimate quality, in the 1820s and especially in the 1830s they showed a tendency to flamboyant, theatrical effects. In the 1820s formal portraiture became fashionable again. Its most prominent representative in Russian painting of the first half of the nineteenth century was undoubtedly **Karl Briullov** (1799–1852). His works, like paintings by other brilliant painters – Orest Kiprensky, Alexander Ivanov, Fiodor Bruni and Sylvester Shchedrin – are exhibited in the imposing interiors of the second floor. It is not a mere coincidence that the largest display rooms in the Russian Museum, Nos 14 and 15, are called "Academic Halls" — they feature perhaps the most brilliant period in the life of the Academy of Arts.

There are many highly impressive large-scale portraits in Briullov's creative heritage. One of such masterpieces is his **Portrait of the Shishmarev Sisters**.

Karl Briullov, famous as a portrait painter, was entrusted to design painted decoration in several major cathedrals and churches. However, he won general renown mainly as a history painter. **The Last Day of Pompeii** is not only the most important work in Briullov's *oeuvre*, but it towers over contemporary Russian painting as a whole. Briullov worked on it more than five years having produced a great deal of sketches and several preliminary painted versions. The completed painting was shown in Rome, Milan and Paris and enjoyed a great success. Brought to St Petersburg, it was displayed with a triumph in the Academy of Arts. *The Last Day of Pompeii* has belonged to the Russian Museum from its first days and is an example, rare in Russia, of the accomplishment of a historically based Romantic concept. The artist focuses on the behaviour and states of the Pompeiians during the dramatic moment. Resolving the tragic, typically Romantic theme in a heightened emotional and colouristic key, the artist endows it with a lofty message.

Fiodor Bruni (1799–1875), Briullov contemporary, expressed his world view in a different way. The biblical episode describing a dramatic situation in the life of the Jewish people was interpreted by Bruni in his painting *The Brazen Serpent* (1841). The painting is dominated by a feeling of dismal gloom probably echoing the moods of some part of society in the 1840s. *The Brazen Serpent*, measuring 565 by 852 cm, is perhaps the museum's largest easel painting produced in the first half of the nineteenth century. Like Briullov, Bruni painted his masterpiece in Italy. He created there some other paintings, now also in the Russian Museum, which are more optimistic in their tonality. Briullov's *Death of Camilla, Sister of the Horatii* (1824) is a typical example of European history painting.

One cannot help noticing a brilliant schooling that distinguishes the work of Bruni, Briullov and other masters of the period. The superb draughtsmanship and mastery of design enabled the artists of that age to handle the most sophisticated

GRIGORY SOROKA. 1823–1864
Fishermen. Second half
of the 1840s
Oil on canvas. 67 x 102

The Pink Tea Service
First half of the 1820s
The Imperial Porcelain
Factory, St Petersburg
Porcelain, painted in colours
over a glaze, gilded and cirrated
Diameter of tray 33.5

IVAN AIVAZOVSKY. 1817–1900
The Tenth Wave. 1850
Oil on canvas. 221 x 332

PAVEL FEDOTOV. 1815–1852
*The Major's Marriage
Proposal (Inspection
of a Prospective Bride
in a Merchant's House)*
Ca 1851
Oil on canvas. 56 x 76

patterns and foreshortenings without any visible effort. Historical paintings and sculptures of the 1830s and 1840s combined Romantic moods with attempts to attain compositional harmony and idealization of the scene represented according to classical examples in keeping with the tenets of Academic art.

The St Petersburg Academy of Arts, with its adherence to classical ancient ideals, rigidly imposed its precepts on students in the late eighteenth and early nineteenth century. Even the most remarkable and talented artists such as **Alexander Ivanov** (1806–1858) were captives of the Academic principles for a long time. Ivanov's painting *The Appearance of Christ to the People* is an epoch-making landmark in the history

of Russian art. It took the artist more than thirty years to complete it — practically he worked on it throughout his artistic career. The painting is based on the Romantic idea of a sudden awareness. While implementing his concept, Ivanov chose a symbolic situation from the history of mankind — the moment of Christ's arrival to the people, the turning of a myth into reality — which might have different interpretations. It was precisely various "states" and moods of the people in connection with the appearance of Jesus Christ that Ivanov was seeking so hard and long to convey. In the process of his work on this immense painting he produced a large amount of study-like portraits, landscapes and compositional sketches which are works of art in their own right.

The version of *The Appearance of Christ to the People* which can be seen in the Russian Museum is a large sketch which had preceded the final variant of the painting now in the Tretyakov Gallery. Alexander Ivanov painted his work in Italy during the 1820s and early 1850s. Some of his studies of figures and landscapes for the painting now in the Russian Museum help understand the artist's tormenting quest for an adequate expression of the religious idea.

The 1820s and 1830s were marked by radical changes in Russian artistic life. By this time the system of a division of the visual arts according to their subject matter which had begun to shape in the preceding century was basically formed. Portraits, landscapes, still lifes as well as historical, battle, interior and everyday life scenes are widely represented in the museum's collection. The visitor will hardly fail to notice a gradual increase in their stylistic and thematic variety.

A sharp contrast to sensitive, impetuous, pathetic heroes in a Romantic vein was made by the contemplative characters created by Alexei Venetsianov, Vasily Tropinin, Nikifor Krylov and Grigory Soroka which began to appear during the same period as works by the Romantic artists and are

PAVEL FEDOTOV. 1815–1852
***Portrait of Nadezhda Zhdanovich
at the Piano.*** 1849
Oil on canvas. 24.5 x 19.2

ALEXANDER IVANOV. 1806–1858
The Appearance of Christ to the People
1836 – not earlier than 1855
Oil on canvas. 172 x 247

hung in the museum side by side with them. These artists captured mostly poetic scenes of daily life in the Russian village featuring landlords or landladies and their peasants. Withdrawn from the turmoil of life, they lived amidst common and habitual things, in complete union with the modest beauty of the Russian countryside.

By that time the conservative cast of the St Petersburg Academy of Arts began to hinder the development of the burgeoning artistic aspirations. The graduates of the Academy, who spent in it ten to fifteen years from early childhood, had a poor knowledge of real life. Possessing thorough schooling as they were, in most cases they still failed to overcome the conventional principles inculcated upon them by classical education. Their observations of real life looked like theatrical performances. Another shortcoming of the

Academy of Arts was its restrictions — for example serf peasants were not given admission to it. This led to the emergence of the first private art school organized and supervised by the aforementioned painter **Alexei Venetsianov** (1780–1847). He gathered around himself talented young artists, including serfs, who were eager to study painting.

In 1821 Venetsianov saw in the Hermitage the painting *The Choir in the Church of the Capuchin Monastery on Piazza Barberini in Rome* by François-Marius Granet. The Russian artist was so struck by the "natural" light and air medium in Granet's work that he decided to attain similar effects in his own paintings. He left St Petersburg for the countryside and indulged in studying nature and everyday life of peasants. One of the first works he sent to an exhibition in St Petersburg was the painting ***Threshing-Barn***. Having received an impulse from the French painter, Venetsianov independently, by a trial and error method, attained similar results in rendering the light and air which filled the space of the interior. For this purpose he removed the wall of a barn and, sitting outside, painted the scene directly from nature. This work is programmatic for Russian painting.

Venetsianov's opposition to the Academy of Arts had no aggressive character. From time to time he would come to St Petersburg and show his own works and those of his pupils at exhibitions. His disciples chose different careers. Some of them, on completing Venetsianov's course, continued their studies at the Academy or were even sent to Italy to perfect their mastery. The most remarkable achievements, however, are associated with Venetsianov's closest followers, Krylov and Soroka, who focused on subjects from Russian life. The work of the peasant artist **Grigory Soroka** (1823–1864) capture the similarly quiet tenor of Russian provincial life, however different it was with landlords and peasants.

Venetsianov's accomplishments are not limited to the foundation of an art school which yielded many artists. His influence upon Russian art was enormous. It was after displays of works by Venetsianov and his pupils in St Petersburg that many Russian artists felt an urge to study the scenery. These efforts were undoubtedly influenced by the echoes of the Biedermeir with its loving attention to private life, but no less important source for such interest was a natural desire to revive the subjects, motifs and genres which were ignored by the Academy.

This entailed a diversity of trends in Russian art of the 1820s to 1840s. A typical feature of art exhibitions in those years was that immense canvases in a Romantic or Academic spirit were displayed next to intimate paintings showing everyday scenes. The holdings of the Russian Museum cover practically all the facets of artistic life during the period.

Ivan Aivazovsky (1817–1900) is one of the world's most popular marine painters. His legacy consists of a great number of pictures devoted to sea views and created mostly from imagination but on the basis of his real observations of the sea. The collection of the Russian Museum has about forty paintings by Aivazovsky from different periods in his creative career. ***The Tenth Wave*** (1850) is the artist's masterpiece, typifying the Romantic emphasis on the tragic aspect of life and man's eternal hope to subdue the elements.

The first half of the nineteenth century saw the growth of high-quality porcelain and glass ware production in Russia. In that period, in addition to the Imperial Porcelain Factory established back in the eighteenth century, there emerged numerous

IVAN VITALI. 1794–1855
Venus. 1852
Marble. 168 x 59 x 64

ALEXANDER IVANOV
1806–1858
Three Nude Boys
1840s–1850s
Oil on canvas. 47.7 x 64.5

ALEXANDER IVANOV
1806–1858
Nude Boy. 1840s–1850s
Oil on canvas. 47.7 x 64.2

private enterprises which catered for the country's needs in tableware. The collection of decorative and applied art is the museum's distinctive feature which makes it different, for example, from the Tretyakov Gallery where this kind of art is not represented.

Unfortunately nowadays, due to a shortage of room, only a small part of the museum's rich holdings is put on display (chandeliers, mosaics, tapestries and furniture in the eighteenth-century rooms; as well as furniture and vases in the White Hall). But on the completion of restoration work in the newly received palaces they will occupy a prominent place at their exhibitions. So far porcelain, glass, furniture, textiles and other items of decorative and applied art can be seen only at temporary exhibitions. These works not only attest to the high technical level and brilliant mastery of their creators, but are also evocative of daily pursuits of various strata of the Russian population, changes in their tenor of life, views on the world, ethic and aesthetic standards.

At the turn of the 1840s and 1850s the situation in the fine arts, similarly to that in literature, began to change. Dramatic or even tragic notes started to intrude

VASILY PEROV. 1834–1882
Solitary Guitar Player. 1865
Oil on panel. 31.2 x 22

VASILY PEROV. 1834–1882
Meal. 1865–1876
Oil on canvas. 84 x 126

NIKOLAI GAY. 1831–1894
**Peter the Great
Interrogating Tsarevich
Alexis at Peterhof.** 1872
Oil on canvas. 134.5 x 173

ALEXEI SAVRASOV. 1830–1897
Rainbow. 1875
Oil on canvas. 45 x 56.5

more and more persistently into the soft lyrical tonality of quiet genre scenes. **Pavel Fedotov** (1815–1852) introduced in painting, like Nikolai Gogol and Fiodor Dostoyevsky in literature, subjects devoted to the life of the so-called third estate — servicemen, officials and various urban employees. The anecdotal situations represented by Fedotov are not merely narrative scenes. Nearly each of his "anecdotes" has a social implication. In one of his central canvases, *The Major's Marriage Proposal* (*ca* 1851), versions of which can be found in the Russian Museum and the Tretyakov Gallery, the artist narrates, with a light irony, a story about a bankrupt officer, a nobleman, who proposes, so as to improve his economic conditions, to a young girl from a merchant family, whose intention is, in turn, to rise higher in their social standing.

Fedotov's work, and after him some other genre painters of the 1840s and 1850s, linked the first and second halves of the nineteenth century. Subjects from daily life became increasingly popular with painters and sculptors in those years. However, the Academy's authorities still continued to persist in their encouragement of mythological, biblical and allegorical subjects limiting a degree of verisimilitude. Konstantin Flavitsky's *Christian Martyrs at the Colosseum* (1862) is a typical example of academic painting of the period.

A remonstrance against the derivative character and formality of the Academy's doctrines, ripening for several decades, burst out in 1861 as a revolt by a group of its graduates. They refused to paint a mythological subject as an examination work and abandoned the Academy. The "dissidents" created the Artel, or the first artistic and commercial union of anti-academic creative forces. The programme worked out by its participants was oriented towards the reflection of real life collisions and it quickly gained popular success. The new form of contacts with viewers by organizing travelling art exhibitions in different cities all over Russia greatly enlarged the society's audience and popularity. In 1870 the Society of Travelling Art Exhibitions was formed which would exist for more than four decades. The realist artists, who joined this society, became known as the Peredvizhniki or Wanderers. Their works well

ILYA REPIN. 1844–1930
Leo Tolstoy with Bare Feet. 1901
Oil on canvas. 207 x 73

ILYA REPIN. 1844–1930
On a Turf Bench. 1876
Oil on canvas. 36 x 55.5

FIODOR KAMENSKY. 1836–1913
Young Sculptor. 1866
Marble. 112 X 47 X 37

IVAN KRAMSKOY. 1837–1887
Mina Moiseyev. 1882
Oil on canvas. 57 x 45

corresponded to the democratic mood of society and to the critical wave which surged the country in that period. This period was marked by the creation of such notable works as **Meal** (1865–76), **Solitary Guitar Player** (1865) and *Orphan Children at a Cemetery* (1864) by **Vasily Perov**, *The Policemen Singing Alleluia* (1867) by Leonid Solomatkin, *Before the Marriage* (1874) and *Begging Children* by Firs Zhuravlev. Independently of these artists' formal membership in the society, they all expressed the democratic ideas proclaimed by the union. The questions *What Is to Be Done?* put by Nikolai Chernyshevsky in his novel of the same name and *Who Is to Blame?* asked a little earlier by Alexander Herzen in the title of his work, were widely discussed by the intelligentsia whose ideals were shared by Russian painters.

These problems can be observed in many paintings containing social criticism in the collection of the Russian Museum. The interpretation of the Gospel story associated with the Last Supper by **Nikolai Gay** (1831–1894) in the light of the 1860s had a sensational success with visitors at the 1863 exhibition in the St Petersburg Academy of Arts. The treatment of historical scenes as real events became usual with the Peredvizhniki. **Peter the Great Interrogating Tsarevich Alexis at Peterhof** by Nikolai Gay, **The Zaporozhye Cossacks** by **Ilya Repin** (1844–1930), *The Conquer of Siberia by Yermak* (1895) and **Alexander Suvorov's Army Crossing the Alps in 1799** (1899) by **Vasily Surikov** (1848–1916) — these are but a few most prominent historical paintings produced by the Peredvizhniki artists. It is remarkable that most of the Peredvizhniki tended to a psychological insight into historical subjects, seeking to interpret the situation depicted through emotional reactions of the participants in the scene. It was not a mere coincidence that all the artists of the second

ILYA REPIN. 1844–1930
*Barge Haulers
on the Volga.* 1870–1873
Oil on canvas. 131.5 x 281

MARK ANTOKOLSKY
1842–1902
Ivan the Terrible. 1871
Bronze. 147 x 100 x 119

ILYA REPIN. 1844–1930
*Portrait of the Writer
and Lawyer Alexander
Zhirkevich.* 1891
Black chalk and charcoal
on paper. 40.9 x 29.8

ILYA REPIN. 1844–1930
*The Zaporozhye
Cossacks.* 1880–1891
Oil on canvas. 203 x 358

half of the nineteenth century who treat-ed historical subjects were fine portrait painters. The collection of the Russian Museum owns a number of portraits by Vasily Perov, Nikolai Gay, Ivan Kramskoi, Nikolai Yaroshenko (1846–1898) and other Peredvizhniki artists.

The range of genres and thematic preferences in the work of the Peredvizh-niki was extremely wide and varied. The 1860s and 1870s witnessed an active struggle of the People's Will, an illegal society of the Populist movement. It con-sisted of representatives of the intelligen-tsia who made their principal aim in life a struggle for the interests of poor and oppressed people. Their "going into the people", mass meetings and terrorist acts ended for most of political figures with imprisonment, exile or death. It was not

ILYA REPIN. 1844–1930
**Formal Session of the State Council in Honour of Its Centenary
on 7 May 1901.** 1903
Oil on canvas. 400 x 877

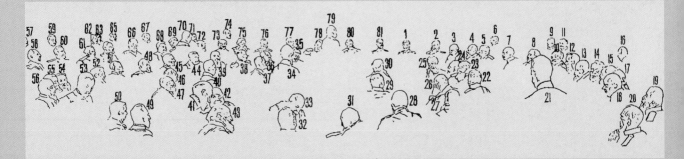

1. Nicholas II
2. Grand Duke Mikhail Nikolayevich
3. Dmitry Solsky
4. Eduard Frisch
5. Admiral Nikolai Chikhachev
6. Sergei Rukhlov
7. Dmitry Nabokov
8. Nikolai Ganetsky
9. N. A. Korevo
10. Count Nikolai Ignatyev
11. Vasily Vereshchagin
12. Count Konstantin Pahlen
13. Piotr Salomon
14. Alexander Polovtsov
15. Christopher Roop
16. Piotr Kharitonov
17. Vladimir Markus
18. Nikolai Mansurov
19. Otton Richter
20. Nikolai Obruchev
21. Prince Dmitry Golitsyn
22. Illarion Vorontsov-Dashkov
23. Ivan Kakhanov
24. Count Alexander Bobrinsky
25. Prince Mikhail Volkonsky
26. Baron Maxim Taube
27. Vladimir Veshniakov
28. Alexander Goremykin
29. Baron Alexander Ikskul von Gildebrandt
30. Nikolai Shebeko
31. Nikolai Makhotin
32. Iliodor Rosing
33. Anatoly Ivashchenkov
34. Baron Yuly Ikskul von Gildebrandt
35. Nikolai Muravyev
36. Count Vladimir Lamsdorf
37. Pavel Gudim-Levkovich
38. Pavel Tyrtov
39. Dmitry Sipiaghin
40. Ivan Golubev
41. Baron Roman Disterlo
42. Alexander Ignatyev
43. Piotr Semenov (Semenov Tien-Shansky)
44. Ivan Shamshin
45. Andrei Saburov
46. Piotr Saburov
47. Nikolai Petrov
48. Nikolai Bobrikov
49. Mikhail Galkin-Vraskoi
50. Baron Vladimir Mengden
51. Fiodor Terner
52. Oskar Kremer
53. Count Andrei Bobrinsky
54. Ivan Goremykin
55. Nikolai Gerard
56. Pavel Markov
57. Alexei Sokov
58. Vladimir Frederiks
59. Alexander Vergopulo
60. Alexei Kuropatkin
61. Pavel Lobko
62. M. F. Pozemkovsky
63. Vladimir Gurko
64. Prince Mikhail Khilkov
65. Dmitry Liubimov
66. Sergei Witte
67. Alexander von Timrot
68. Alexei Yermolov
69. Nikolai Protasov-Bakhmetev
70. Vladimir Lyshchinsky
71. Nikolai Deriuzhinsky
72. Piotr Vannovsky
73. Konstantin Pobedonostsev
74. Dmitry Filosofov
75. Ivan Durnovo
76. Prince Alexander Oldenburgsky
77. Grand Duke Sergei Alexandrovich
78. Grand Duke Alexei Alexandrovich
79. Viacheslav Plehwe
80. Grand Duke Vladimir Alexandrovich
81. Grand Duke Mikhail Alexandrovich

accidental therefore that images of revolutionaries occur frequently in the art of the period, notably in such works as *The Convict* (1879) by Vladimir Makovsky (1846–1920) and *A Girl Student* (1880) by Nikolai Yaroshenko. The Peredvizhniki artists concentrated their attention on scenes of poverty and destitution — *The Doss-House* (1889) by Vladimir Makovsky, *They Became Orphans* (1891) by Nikolai Kasatkin and many other paintings. They did not neglect, however, more optimistic subjects including happiness and love — **On the Swing** (1888) by **Nikolai Yaroshenko**, *Dreams about the Future* (1868) by Vasily Maximov, **The Taking of a Snow Fortress** (1891) by **Vasily Surikov**, etc.

One of the most popular figures among the Peredvizhniki was Ilya Repin. His art is represented in the Russian Museum by many works from various periods beginning with his earliest essays as an artist. One of culminating accomplishments in his artistic career is the picture **Barge Haulers on the Volga** painted between 1870 and 1873. Repin treated the theme of hard slavish labour in a concise, simple and powerful manner, and the painting became a pictorial symbol of the age. The composition skilfully unites about ten incisive portraits, but Repin did not stop at that — his *Barge Haulers* cannot be regarded merely as a group portrait or a genre scene. This painting is a telling metaphor

NIKOLAI YAROSHENKO
1846–1898
On the Swing. 1888
Oil on canvas. 58.3 x 40.5

FIODOR VASILYEV. 1850–1873
View of the Volga: Boats
1870
Oil on canvas. 67 x 105

IVAN SHISHKIN. 1832–1898
The Mast-Tree Grove. 1898
Oil on canvas. 165 x 252

GRIGORY MIASOYEDOV
1834–1911
**Harvest Time
(Mowers).** 1887
Oil on canvas. 179 x 275

of physical force and a lack of power, love for freedom and inability to tear off the bonds of slavery. After appearing at exhibitions in the 1870s this picture immediately attracted the general attention of the public and critics.

Among the most notable works possessed by the Russian Museum is its largest painting, *Formal Session of the State Council in Honour of Its Centenary on 7 May 1901* (1903), which was painted by **Ilya Repin with a group of his pupils**. The painting used to adorn the main hall of the Mariinsky Palace in St Petersburg. The group portrait of more than eighty characters demanded a large amount of preliminary work. Repin himself portrayed the majority of members of the State Council (his studies are also in the Russian Museum). Repin, a talented psychologist, sought not only to convey the outward features of the well-known statesmen, but revealed a keen insight into the individual characters of the senators who were to decide the destinies of Russia.

Many artists active in the latter half of the nineteenth century showed a growing attention to national features — Russian history, life and nature. Local landscape scenes began

ARKHIP KUINJI. 1842(?)–1910
Rainbow. 1900–05
Oil on canvas. 110 x 171

ARKHIP KUINJI. 1842(?)–1910
Evening in Ukraine. 1878
Oil on canvas. 81 x 163

ISAAC LEVITAN. 1860–1900
**The Golden Autumn:
A Settlement.** 1889
Oil on canvas. 43 x 67.2

ISAAC LEVITAN. 1860–1900
The Lake. 1899–1900
Oil on canvas. 149 x 208

VASILY SURIKOV. 1848–1916
Alexander Suvorov's
Army Crossing the Alps
in 1799. 1899
Oil on canvas. 495 x 373

VICTOR VASNETSOV. 1848–1926
Knight
at the Crossroads. 1882
Oil on canvas. 167 x 299

HENRYK SIEMIRADZKI. 1843–1902
Phryne at the Poseidon
Celebration in Eleusis. 1889
Oil on canvas. 390 x 763.5

to attract painters more and more often during that period. **Alexei Savrasov** (1830–1897) made the emphasis on the poetic aspects of the Russian countryside never noticed before. The works of **Ivan Shishkin** (1832–1898) were remarkable for the poetic perception of the forest. Upon his graduation from the College of Painting, Sculpture and Architecture he studied at the Academy of Arts. In 1862 the Academy sent the promising artist to study abroad as its pensioner. He lived and worked in Düsseldorf. On return home, Shishkin wrote in his diary: "My motto? To be a Russian. Long live Russia!" Seeking to recreate the scenery as exactly as possible, he carefully studied nature. Many of his paintings contain a detailed observation of man's natural environment (e.g. *The Mast-Tree Grove*, 1898). However, Shishkin could hardly be blamed for a primitively naturalistic approach. Among his studies there occur true masterpieces notable for their poetic evocation of nature (*Goutweed: Pargolovo*, 1884–85). Such Shishkin's paintings in the

Female costume. Late 19th century
Sapozhkovo District, Ryazan Region
Embroidery in wool on sateen

Hand-painted tray. 1870s. Zhostovo,
Moscow Region, Workshop of
Osip Vishniakov & Sons
Lacquered decorative painting in oils
on metal. 46.5 x 59.5 x 2.5

VASILY SURIKOV. 1848–1916
The Taking of a Snow Fortress. 1891
Oil on canvas. 156 x 282

Distaffs. Mid-19th – early 20th centuries
Vologda Region
Wood, carved and painted

collection of the Russian Museum paintings as *Oaks* (1887), *Winter* (1890) or *Near the Shores of the Gulf of Finland* (1889) are lyrical and at the same time faithful images of the Russian countryside.

The treatment of landscape scenes in Russian painting during the second half of the nineteenth century had something in common with an approach to nature in contemporary Russian literature. The artists and writers focused their attention not only on the outward elements of reality. They used the states of nature to convey their thoughts and to observe an emotional atmosphere of the environment. Thus, a fresh approach to a trivial subject resulted in the creation of such charming canvas as *The Moscow Courtyard* (1902) by **Vasily Polenov** (1844–1927). This heartfelt painting is a veritable pictorial novella about a cozy corner of Moscow.

Polenov was not a landscape painter. Like many other artists during that period, he painted historical paintings (*The Arrest of a Huguenot Jacobine de Montebel*, 1875); biblical subjects (**Christ and the Woman Taken in Adultery**, 1888), genre and landscape scenes. This versatility marks a general tendency in the evolution of art during the second half of the nineteenth century. Historical or biblical motifs became more impressive when they were interpreted in a life-like manner — they ceased to be just views inspired by the artist's emotional or philosophical attitude to nature.

Landscape painting in general had a wealth and variety of forms in Russian art during the second half of the nineteenth century. Its strong Romantic traditions were shaped by Ivan Aivazovsky, Alexei Savrasov and **Fiodor Vasilyev** (1850–1873). Works by **Arkhip Kuinji** (1842–1910) are notable among them for their unusual colouristic perception. Moreover, Kuinji introduced into the landscape of the 1870s and 1880s that measure of convention and terseness which would appear in Russian art only at the turn of the nineteenth and twentieth century. He was not interested in objects of the material world alone. Kuinji was primarily concerned with light and colour effects in different hours of day and night, in winter and summer.

Isaac Levitan (1860–1900) occupies a place of his own among landscape painters of the second half of the nineteenth century. His works are often justly compared to the prose of Anton Chekhov. The artist and the writer were good friends and their views had really much in common.

Levitan's work was characterized by quests for the "soul of Russian nature". His paintings are not just typical views of certain places. The artist expressed his creative personality in "mood landscapes" which would convey a whole gamut of feelings — from joy to sorrow, from pessimistic overtones to overtly optimistic mood. Levitan's best works in the collection

of the Russian Museum also convey profound thoughts on the life and man in terms of nature (**The Golden Autumn: A Settlement**, 1889; *Spring: The Last Snow*, 1894; *Twilight: Moonshine*, 1899; **The Lake**, 1899–1900).

The late nineteenth and early twentieth century were a turbulent period in the history of Russian art. Those years saw the emergence and development of diverse artistic trends. Such artists as **Abram Arkhipov** (1862–1930) (*Laundresses*, 1901) and Nikolai Kasatkin (1859–1930) (*They Became Orphans*, 1891; *Poor People Gathering Coal at a Worked-Out Mine*, 1894) continued to treat social themes following in the footsteps of the Peredvizhniki. Others, like **Vasily Vereshchagin** (1842–1904) chose an independent way of their own having no traditions in Russian painting. Vereshchagin travelled much and saw action. His paintings, including the works in the Russian Museum collection, deal with war and human tragedies associated with it (*Shipka-Sheinovo,* before 1890) or concentrate on specific features of daily life in various countries (**At the Door of a Mosque**, 1873; *Jerusalem: Royal Tombs*, 1884/5).

One of the most interesting features characteristic of Russian art at the turn of the century was a change in an attitude to national history. Not only historical subjects, but also tales, anecdotes and stories based on events from Russian history began to serve as sources of inspi-

VASILY POLENOV. 1844–1927
Christ and the Woman Taken in Adultery (Who Has No Sin?). 1888
Oil on canvas. 325 x 611

VASILY VERESHCHAGIN 1842–1904
At the Door of a Mosque 1873
Oil on canvas. 315.5 x 237.5

MARK ANTOKOLSKY. 1842–1902
Mermaid. 1900
Marble. 59 x 42 x 30

VASILY POLENOV. 1844–1927
In the Park: The Village of Veuilles in Normandy. 1874
Oil on canvas. 61 x 46

ration for a group of major Russian artists. One of them, **Victor Vasnetsov** (1848–1926) derived subjects for his paintings such as *The Knight at the Crossroads* (1882) and *Bayan* (1910) from Russian epic tales. His characters can be immediately recognized as Russians for their distinctly national features. **Andrei Riabushkin** (1861–1904) concentrated on everyday scenes from the past — *A Street in Seventeenth-Century Moscow* (1895), *A Seventeenth-Century Merchant Family* (1896), etc. A slight touch of humour inherent to Riabushkin's view of Russian daily life, was opposed to pathetic treatment typical of historical painting. This new approach was shared by several other masters. **Boris Kustodiev** (1878–1927) poeticized the life of the middle-class inhabitants of a provincial town (*A Merchant's Wife*, 1915; *Shrovetide*, 1916; *A Merchant's Wife at Tea*, 1918). **Philip Maliavin*** (1869–1940) enjoyed world renown for his depictions of Russian peasant women in bright-coloured

sarafans and head-kerchiefs, which became an epitome of cheerfulness and elemental energy. Maliavin's riotous colour solutions perfectly match the subject matter of his paintings tinged with a national flavour. **Nicholas Roerich** (1874–1947) also often borrowed themes from Russian history. It is worth mentioning here that Kustodiev, Maliavin and Roerich were Repin's students. The Russian Museum owns a number of their works from the period when they had been stylistically closer to their teacher imitating Repin's realistic portrayal of the world.

A rupture of Repin's pupils with the traditions of the Peredvizhniki and their efforts to evolve their own ways mark the widening of the artistic scene in Russia at the turn of the nineteenth and twentieth centuries. The closer we come to the time of crucial social changes the tenser are relations between man and society, the artist and the object of his creative work. And while the beginning of the nineteenth century was characterized in Russian painting by an unhurried development of unified, lofty and austere aesthetic canons of Classicism, art at the turn of the next, twentieth century was pregnant with a presentiment of social catastrophes and a denunciation of ideals.

---

* The creative work of Abram Arkhipov, Boris Kustodiev, Philip Maliavin and Nicholas Roerich flourished in the early 20th century and therefore their paintings are reproduced in the next section.

Russian Art
of the 20th Century

The turn of the nineteenth and twentieth centuries was the time of flowering of Art Nouveau, a style which became widespread simultaneously in Europe and Russia. This style opened up unusually large possibilities of both customary and novel materials used in the fine arts in imitation of the whimsical forms of nature. The artists' refined fantasy rapidly took them away from all customary and usual, and the world of nature, reflected in the mirror of art, turned into an elaborate and elegant ornament, a whimsical decorative combination of colours, volumes and rhythms. Emphasis on a sinuous line, an almost morbid distortion of form and a shimmering of light — these are distinctive stylistic features of Art Nouveau.

A survey of twentieth-century art in the Russian Museum begins from the hall where works by Mikhail Vrubel, an artist of stature, are displayed (the Benois Block, Room 66). This part of the exhibition includes not only twentieth-century paintings — many of the canvases were produced earlier. However, in order not to break apart the displays of major artists, such as Mikhail Nesterov, Boris Kustodiev, Valentin Serov and others, the works of each of them are concentrated within a single period section.

Mikhail Vrubel (1856–1910) began his artistic career at the end of the nineteenth century, like some other artists whose works are displayed in the twentieth-century section. He often turned to literary subjects, fairy-tale and *bylina* (epic-tale) themes (***The Bogatyr***, 1898, *Hamlet and Ophelia*, 1884), similarly to many of his contemporaries. However, the artistic idiom of Vrubel's works goes far beyond the bounds of the imagery characteristic of the nineteenth century. The exaggerated figure of the Russian *bogatyr* or knight, the frankly decorative treatment of the landscape and the untraditional format distinguish *The Bogatyr* among the fairy-tale subjects painted by his contemporaries.

The modelling of form by means of brushstrokes similar to tesserae in his *Six-Winged Seraphim* (1904), a terse and ultimately conventional depiction of the sea and warriors in *Thirty-Three Bogatyrs* (1901) suggest an artistic system of rendering reality or an imaginary realm different from that accepted in the nineteenth century. Vrubel destroys the classical notions of form and composition. The Demon is one of central themes in Vrubel's art. His major works on this subject, *The Demon Seated* (1890) and *The Demon Downcast* (1902), are at the Tretyakov Gallery in Moscow. Several illustrations to Lermontov's

VALENTIN SEROV. 1865–1911
Portrait of Ida Rubinstein
1910
Tempera and charcoal on
canvas. 147 x 233

MIKHAIL VRUBEL. 1856–1910
The Bogatyr. 1898
Decorative panel
Oil on canvas. 321.5 x 222

poem *The Demon* and the painting **The Demon in Flight** (1899) can be seen in the Russian Museum. *The Demon in Flight*, like some other Vrubel's works, is associated with the ideas of Symbolism. The creation of the new symbolic idiom implementing spiritual quests is a characteristic symptom of Russian art at the turn of the centuries. Vrubel's Demon, like Lermontov's, is "suffering and sorrowful, imperious and majestic". His horizontally stretched figure hangs over the earth. The inflamed, fiery eyes peep attentively down trying to discern what is going on there.

Valentin Serov (1865–1911) was Mikhail Vrubel's fellow student in the workshop of Pavel Chistiakov at the Moscow College of Painting, Sculpture and Architecture. His early works may be classified as Impressionistic (*Portrait of Adelaida Simonovich*, 1889). Further on he steadily developed the main tradition of Western European and Russian art enriching it with his quests for colour and light along the lines of Impressionism.

Serov painted subtle lyrical landscapes (*In Winter*, 1898), historical compositions (**Peter II and Tsesarevna Elisabeth Riding to Hounds**, 1900) and scenes which are difficult to place in some definite category (*Children*, 1899). But the most brilliant facet of Serov's art are portraits. They are different in dimensions, composition and colour scheme. Serov was ruthless to his sitters. Neither a luxurious setting nor splendid dresses could conceal the artist's attitude to his models. Serov's formal portraits show Sophia Botkina (1899), Felix Yusupov (1903) and Olga Olrova (1911) as cold society people. Countess Orlova was so disappointed with her likeness commissioned from Serov, although it was the artist's veritable masterpiece, that she hastened to get rid of it — in 1912 she presented it to the Russian Museum.

In 1907 Valentin Serov in the company of another artist, Leon Bakst, went to Greece. This travel turned out to have a decisive influence on Serov's art. He was infatuated with archaic art, Greek and Egyptian reliefs and decorative paintings. The portraits Serov produced during the last years of his short lifetime were executed in a completely different style than those created before. In some of them (*The Rape of Europa*, 1910) one can sense the echo of Symbolism, while others (e.g. **Portrait of Ida Rubinstein**, 1910) suggest an affinity with Matisse. The portrait of Ida Rubinstein, a ballerina who became famous for several major parts in Diaghilev's Russian Seasons, by its economy of colour and line is reminiscent of a poster or drawing. The artist discards the careful rendering of details of the environment concentrating on the

MIKHAIL VRUBEL. 1856–1910
The Demon in Flight
1899. Unfinished
Oil on canvas. 138.5 x 430.5

MIKHAIL VRUBEL. 1856–1910
After a Concert
Black pastel, black and white
chalk. 44.2 x 39.5

angular plasticity of the body to convey the essence of the celebrated dancer.

Konstantin Korovin (1861–1939), who was a contemporary and friend of both Vrubel and Serov, continued the Impressionist trend in art. In the Russian Museum Korovin's landscapes and still lifes, remarkable for their pictorial merits, hang next to his theatrical designs, decorative panels and portraits. Usually Korovin portrayed people well known to him. With Tatyana Liubatovich, an opera singer who performed the leading parts in Savva Mamontov's Private Opera, Korovin made friends at Abramtsevo, Mamontov's country estate near Moscow. At the end of the nineteenth century, Abramtsevo was a prominent art centre where writers, artists and actors used to gather. The place was frequented by Korovin, Vrubel, Serov and others. Korovin's *Portrait of Tatyana Liubatovich* is not just a depiction of a concrete individual — it is the quintessence of femininity, freshness and inspiration. The imposing Fiodor Chaliapin appears no less light-hearted and merry in Korovin's portrait painted in 1911.

However, the art life of the period was by no means characterized by an idyllic

VICTOR BORISOV-MUSATOV. 1870–1905
Self-Portrait with a Sister. 1898
Oil on canvas. 143 x 177

VALENTIN SEROV. 1865–1911
*Peter II and Tsesarevna Elizabeth
Petrovna Riding to Hounds.* 1900
Tempera and gouache on paper mounted
on cardboard. 41 x 39

VALENTIN SEROV. 1865–1911
*Portrait of Princess
Zinaida Yusupova.* 1902
Oil on canvas. 181.5 x 133

ALEXANDER BENOIS
1870–1960
**Versailles: The Venetian
Garden.** 1910
Watercolour, gouache and
white on cardboard. 48.4 x 63.7

LÉON BAKST. 1866–1924
Terror Antiquus. 1908
Oil on canvas. 250 x 270

KONSTANTIN SOMOV
1869–1939
**Colombine Poking
Her Tongue.** 1915
Watercolour and gouache
on cardboard. 29.2 x 22.5

calm and balance. Passions were getting increasingly strained due to the confrontation between the members of the Travelling Art Exhibitions, who regarded art as a "textbook of life" and sought to take an active social stand castigating the vices of contemporary society, and another group of artists who proclaimed a proud seclusion in an "ebony tower" and tried to create a magnificent imaginary world, alien to fleeting immediate concerns, and oriented towards the past.

The most prominent creative group representing the second trend was the World of Art, a society which received its name from the magazine published by its members. The society and its magazine played an important role in the history of Russian culture at the turn of the nineteenth and early twentieth centuries. Events from the history of Europe

and Russia and scenes of daily life were vividly recreated in elegant and somewhat stylized works by **Alexander Benois** (1870–1960), **Yevgeny Lanceray** (1875–1946), **Konstantin Somov** (1869–1939) and **Mstislav Dobuzhinsky** (1875–1957), whose work is amply represented in the collection of the Russian Museum. ***Versailles: The Venetian Garden*** by Benois capturing the royal residence of the French kings is a typical landscape scene of this highly educated artist reflecting his interest in the history of world culture and emphasis on the aesthetic aspect of art. Somov's fanciful works, such as ***Colombine Poking Her Tongue***, and ***Winter: Skating Rink*** (both 1915), conjure up a vision of an enigmatic world combining a stylized recreation of the past with theatrical effects. ***A Province in the 1830s***, a watercolour by Dobuzhinsky, introduces the viewer into the everyday life of a Russian provincial town in the bygone times.

Members of the World of Art group largely extended the scope of their artistic activities. An important facet of their creative work became book illustration and design — artists of the union greatly raised the standing of these fields of art formerly regarded as auxiliary ones. It was also in the World of Art that an interest of painters in the theatre was developed to become one of their major occupations. Theatrical predilections of the artists who paid much attention to scenography, such as Léon Bakst (1866–1924) or Alexander Golovin (1863–1930), could be sensed even in the style of their easel works. For example, Golovin's portrait of the celebrated bass, **Chaliapin as Boris Godunov in Mussorgsky's Opera of the Same Name**, is characterized by the stylistic devices

KONSTANTIN SOMOV
1869–1939
Winter: Skating Rink. 1915
Oil on canvas. 49 x 58

NICHOLAS ROERICH. 1874–1947
Guests from Overseas. 1902
Oil on cardboard. 79 x 100

MSTISLAV DOBUZHINSKY
1875–1957
A Province in the 1830s
1907–09
Watercolour and graphite
on paper. 60 x 83.5

KONSTANTIN KOROVIN. 1861–1939
**Portrait of Fiodor
Chaliapin.** 1911
Oil on canvas. 65 x 81

ALEXANDER GOLOVIN
1863–1930
**Portrait of Fiodor Chaliapin
as Boris Godunov
in Mussorgsky's Opera
of the Same Name.** 1912
Size colours, gouache, paste
white chalk, gold and silver oil
211.5 x 139.5

YEVGENY LANCERAY. 1875–1946
**St Petersburg in the Early
Eighteenth Century.** 1906
Tempera on paper. 58.5 x 111.5

typical of stage curtain and costume design as are most of
the artist's other works. The painting ***Terror Antiquus*** (1908)
by **Léon Bakst** is also reminiscent of a huge stage curtain,
although his portraits are painted in a different manner (*Supper*, 1902; *Portrait of Sergei Diaghilev with His Nurse*, 1906).
Although not fully traditional, they still retain the spirit of easel compositions.

After the creation of the World of Art new groups began
to emerge on the Russian art scene, each with its own programme and distinctive predilections. A recourse from reality to the world of dreams was characteristic of lyrical, light-
coloured paintings by Victor **Borisov-Musatov** (1870–1905),
a leading figure of the union bearing a poetic name, the Blue
Rose. The subtle and expressive colour range of paintings
by **Pavel Kuznetsov** (1878–1968) — his still lifes, portraits
set in a landscape and romantic scenes from Eastern life —

DMITRY STELLETSKY. 1875–1947
An Aristocratic Boyar Woman. 1910
Wood. 69 x 39 x 30

NIKOLAI SAPUNOV. 1880–1912
Merry-Go-Round. 1908
Tempera on canvas. 146 x 193.5

MIKHAIL NESTEROV. 1862–1942
The Taking of the Veil. 1898
Oil on canvas. 178 x 195

ZINAIDA SEREBRIAKOVA
1884–1967
In a Bath-House. 1913
Oil on canvas. 135 x 174

has something in common with Borisov-Musatov's soft chromatic harmonies.

Another remarkable and quite unusual phenomenon of the early twentieth century was Neo-Classicism or, as it was then called, Neo-Romanticism. **Alexander Yakovlev** (1887–1938, **Vasily Shukhayev** (1887–1973) and **Zinaida Serebriakova** (1884–1967) drew their inspiration from works by mediaeval and Renaissance masters in the period when innovatory formal quests were more fashionable. Like pre-Raphaelites, they treated present-day subjects with the use of a slight stylization drawing on the pictorial and plastic language of great predecessors. Zinaida Serebriakova and **Boris Grigoryev** (1886–1939) revealed a strong interest in the Russian theme.

The beginning of the twentieth century was marked by more direct contacts of Russian artists with modern Western European art. They familiarized themselves with the accomplishments of the world's leading masters during theirs tours of European countries, which became a usual practice in those years. Even never leaving Russia they could have a good idea of them from the collections of Ivan Morozov and Sergei Shchukin. These Russian art collectors began to acquire canvases by Cézanne, Matisse and other pioneers of modern art when they were not yet highly appreciated in the world. Thanks to the fine judgement of Morozov and Shchukin,

they exerted a definite influence on the evolution of the Russian fine arts.

Thus a group of Cézanne's followers appeared in Russia. To shock philistines, they named their union the "Jack of Diamonds". The artists of the group adhered to Cézanne's style, but they transformed it in a specific Russian manner. The still lifes, portraits and landscapes of **Ilya Mashkov** (1881–1944), **Piotr Konchalovsky** (1876–1956), **Alexander Kuprin** (1880–1960) and Aristarkh Lentulov (1882–1943) not only betray the devices borrowed from Cézanne, but drew on the traditions of Russian folklore — shop signs, toys and cheap popular prints with their pictorial plasticity and crude yet expressive subject matter.

A recourse to traditional Russian roots was revealed in a profound and varied manner at the beginning of the twentieth century. Next to bright-coloured, succulent works by Mashkov, Lentulov and Konchalovsky, who relied on popular traditions and motifs, one could see at art exhibitions

PAVEL KUZNETSOV. 1878–1968
Shearing Sheep
Pastel and tempera on canvas
77.5 x 81.5

Kustodiev's buoyant scenes from the everyday life of Russian merchants slightly tinged with humour. In sharp contrast to them were sensitive philosophical works by **Mikhail Nesterov** (1862–1942), an artist deeply concerned with the destiny of Russia. His paintings extol the purity and harmony of ascetic life, laying emphasis on the spiritual qualities characteristic of people who retired from the bustle of worldly life. Nesterov's painting ***The Taking of the Veil*** (1898) capturing an episode from Russian ecclesiastical life is pervaded with a feeling of sublime poetry, bit it also has a touch of serene melancholy about it.

Kuzma Petrov-Vodkin (1878–1939) began his artistic career with an imitation of French Symbolism, but in the 1910s he completely turned to Russian themes and a quest for national expressive means. The artist's main sources of inspiration were Russian icons and the Russian countryside. His works are marked by a great thematic and compositional variety — austere, even ascetic still lifes, portraits and everyday scenes bearing some resemblance to icons, narrative military or everyday scenes based on present-day or historical events in the life of the country.

Thus a powerful stream of works devoted to the past and present of the country and treated in an unusual and different way was produced during the early phase of the twentieth century adding an important facet to the motley art scene of the period.

It was not a mere coincidence that during this period principally new aesthetic ideas began to emerge and mature in Russia: Mikhail Larionov invented Rayonnism; Kasimir Malevich with his associates and followers introduced Suprematism; Abstractionism by Wassily Kandinsky has grown on the soil of excesses of objective art. A new movement which united the artists who declared themselves to be antagonists and destroyers of the past and repudiated all that existed before them — the habitual precepts, canons and dogmas. The radical innovators cast a decisive challenge to other art groups. The Russian avant-garde was emerging on the art scene of the twentieth century.

In contemporary art scholarship this notion is firmly and evidently forever associated with a brief yet extremely fruitful and dramatic period in the history of Russian fine arts — the first three decades of the twentieth century. It was precisely within this period and

ARKADY RYLOV. 1870–1933
Forest River. 1929
Oil on canvas. 86 x 121.9

PHILIP MALIAVIN. 1869–1940
Peasant Women. 1905
Oil on canvas. 205 x 159

ILYA MASHKOV. 1881–1944
Still Life with a Pineapple. 1908
Oil on canvas. 121 x 171

in this sphere of creative work that Russia became the trend-setter discovering new ways which would determine the course of the development of the fine arts throughout the world for several later decades.

The world's largest collection of the Russian avant-garde is the pride of the Russian Museum. Its unique specific feature is that the kernel of this collection is made up of about 500 works selected by the avant-garde masters themselves, including Kandinsky, Malevich, **Mikhail Matiushin** (1861–1934), Vladimir Tatlin and Pavel Mansurov, who tried to create in 1921, in the zeal of revolutionary transformations, an absolutely innovatory kind of museum in Petrograd, the Museum of Artistic Culture, in which, according to Malevich's concept, "an old notion of an artist disappears and is replaced by a scholarly artist." The experiment was completed very quickly for two reasons: first, the strengthening official ideology did not bear the revolutionary games of "scholarly artists" and, second, the pioneering artists themselves turned out to be too distinctive individualities for running in a single harness and quickly quarrelled one with another. As a result the unique collection of avant-garde art was transferred to the Russian Museum in 1926.

The changes which have taken place in the last decade enabled to disclose the "secret" stocks and to show them at last to the general public abandoning the primitive division of Russian art into "pre-revolutionary" and "post-revolutionary" periods.

The art of the avant-garde is the final phase of a certain, probably biological, cycle marked by a tiredness of the public consciousness, a break of routine, maybe sometimes even progressive traditions, a casting down of authorities, a denial of the ideals which turned into stereotypes and dogmas from their too long use.

Repeating in a mirror-like way the situation of the Petrine period, when art shifted from icon-painting to portraiture, early twentieth-century art,

ABRAM ARKHIPOV
1862–1930
Laundresses. 1901
Oil on canvas. 97 x 65.5

ABRAM ARKHIPOV
1862–1930
On a Visit. 1915
Oil on canvas. 105 x 154

NATALIA GONCHAROVA
1881–1962
Laundresses. 1911
Oil on canvas. 102 x 146

MIKHAIL LARIONOV
1881–1964
Venus. 1912
Oil on canvas. 83 x 100

MIKHAIL LARIONOV. 1881–1964
Near a Camp. 1910–1911
Oil on canvas. 72 x 89.5

MIKHAIL LARIONOV. 1881–1964
Hairdresser
Oil on canvas. 77.5 x 59.5

OLGA ROZANOVA. 1886–1918
The Four Aces:
Simultaneous Representation
From the series *Playing Cards*
Oil on canvas. 85 x 67.5

breaking or radically changing real forms, has turned to the icon again (although this time it was perceived as a sign system rather than as a religious object) — in *Black Square* (*ca* 1923) and other works by **Malevich**, *The Holy Family* (1914) by **Filonov** and *The Evangelists* (1910) by Natalia Goncharova.

Represented in the Russian Museum are practically all the trends and movements, all the names of the diversified process of the affirmation of new aesthetic ideas and means of artistic expression. **Mikhail Larionov** (1881–1964) and **Natalia Goncharova** (1881–1962) were perhaps the first to abandon narrative subjects and lay emphasis on simplified forms. Their recourse to folk art of different countries, including Russia and Ukraine, enriched the palette and plastic vocabulary of these masters who made a major contribution to Russian art. Nathan Altman (1889–1970) and Marc Chagall (1887–1985), who traversed a long creative path, began as followers of French Cubism. However, already their early works bear a charge of an absolute creative independence. The best paintings by these artists created in the middle of the 1910s, e.g. *Portrait of Anna Akhmatova* (1914) by **Nathan Altman** and *Promenade* (1917) by **Marc Chagall**, rank with the most famous works of the Russian avant-garde.

Wassily Kandinsky (1866–1944), who went through a phase of Expressionism,

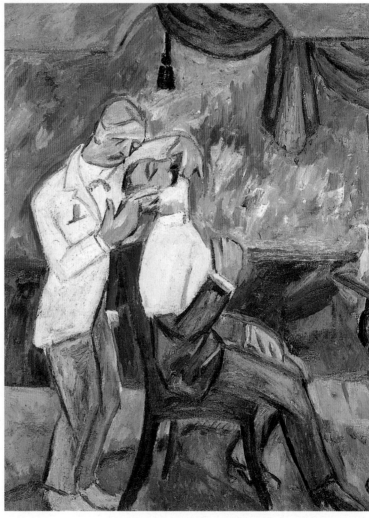

arrived at non-objectivity as his principle in art as early as 1911. The Russian Museum owns more than twenty works by Kandinsky which enable one to trace the artist's creative path from Expressionism to Non-Representational Art. Kandinsky's artistic concepts are based on the subconscious and form is determined by colour, rhythm and spots in his work. He was close to folk craftsmen in that respect. Russian icon-painting also exerted a marked influence on his art.

Kasimir Malevich (1878–1935) arrived at the discovery of Suprematism through Impressionism, Cubism and Cubo-Futurism. His collection in the Russian Museum (more than 100 paintings and 20 drawings) is larger than in any other museum throughout the world. It includes his paintings of the Impressionist and Symbolist periods, the Cubo-Futuristic *Portrait of Kliun* (1911) and *Pilot* (1914), the Suprematist compositions of 1915 and 1916, the large peasant series of 1928–32 which combines Suprematist and figurative elements, as well as works of his later years.

ILYA MASHKOV. 1881–1944
Still Life with a Fan. 1921
Oil on canvas. 145 x 127.5

ALEXANDER KUPRIN
1880–1960
*Still Life with the
Sculpture of Boris
Korolev.* 1919
Oil on canvas. 115 x 120

PIOTR KONCHALOVSKY
1876–1956
Porta Fontebranda. 1912
Oil on canvas. 96.2 x 81

PAVEL FILONOV. 1883–1941
**Peasant Family
(The Holy Family).** 1914
Oil on canvas. 159 x 128

MARC CHAGALL. 1887–1985
Mirror. 1915
Oil on cardboard. 100 x 81

MARC CHAGALL. 1887–1985
Red Jew. 1915
Oil on cardboard. 100 x 80.5

VASILY SHUKHAYEV. 1887–1973
ALEXANDER YAKOVLEV
1887–1938
**Self-Portraits (Harlequin
and Pierrot).** 1914
Oil on canvas. 210 x 142

No less remarkable and complete is the collection of works by **Pavel Filonov** (1883–1941). Nearly 200 paintings and over 200 drawings and watercolours by this artist were presented to the museum by his sister Yevdokia Glebova.

Filonov's distinctive individuality could already be sensed in his early compositions (*Shrovetide*, 1913–14; *The War with Germany*, 1915). Although they suggest his links with folklore, they represent the initial stage of the artist's work at the so-called Analytical Method which he continued to use and develop throughout his mature years.

Filonov was growing his images similarly to the process of growth of plants in nature. His compositions as a rule look like mosaics or pictures in a kaleidoscope. But behind the form itself, original and aesthetically attractive, there lie Filonov's profound philosophical thoughts about man and the surrounding world.

Besides large collections of Malevich and Filonov, the Russian Museum owns paintings and reliefs by **Vladimir Tatlin** (1885–1953), works by **Olga Rozanova** (1885–1918), **Liubov Popova** (1889–1924), Nadezhda Udaltsova (1886–1961), **Alexander Rodchenko** (1891–1956), Ivan Pougny (1894–1956) and many other representatives of the Russian avant-garde of the 1900s–1920s. Unfortunately the present-day display of this innovatory movement in the museum includes not very many works by artists of this circle.

The subsequent development of Russian art, perfectly illustrated in the collection of the Russian Museum, will be opened to spectators gradually, as repair

MARC CHAGALL. 1887–1885
Promenade. 1917
Oil on canvas. 170 x 163.5

KUZMA PETROV-VODKIN
1878–1939
Thirsty Warrior. 1915
Oil on canvas. 65 x 105

ALEXANDER MATVEYEV
1878–1960
Sleeping Boy. 1910
Study for Victor Borisov-
Musatov's tombstone
Tinted plaster of Paris
33 x 143 x 80

and restoration work will be completed. It is, however, important to mention now that these works are kept in the stocks of the Russian Museum.

Undoubtedly, the tragic combination in the new history of Russia of the October Revolution and the two wars, the First World War and the Civil War, could not but become a powerful impetus of the processes then taking place in the country. Bit if to use a cliché about "art born by the October Revolution", it should be applied to the 1930s, the period of "Socialist Realism".

The totalitarian age, the rule of Joseph Stalin, made important transformations in artistic life too, In 1932 a decree was issued which liquidated all creative groupings except for the officially recognized Union of Artists. The so-called Socialist Realism was proclaimed to be the only right and universal method to be followed by all artists without any exclusion. And then an ideological hierarchy began to be established under the keen control of the party and the state which divided all artists into three categories — officially

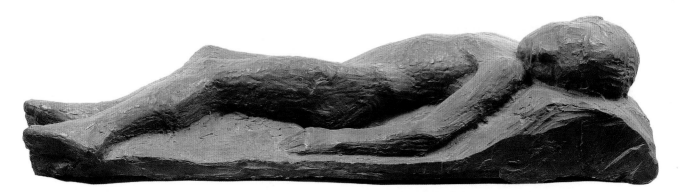

BORIS GRIGORYEV. 1886–1939
In a Carriage. 1913
Graphite on paper. 33.3 x 27.7

NATHAN ALTMAN. 1889–1970
*Portrait of a Young Jew
(Self-Portrait).* 1916
Plaster of Paris, copper and wood
51 x 31 x 27

DAVID STERENBERG. 1881–1948
*Still Life with a Kerosene
Lamp.* Ca 1922
Oil on cardboard. 50 x 36

SAMUIL ADLIVANKIN
1897–1966
The B Tram Route. 1922
Oil on plywood. 47 x 60

recognized, half-recognized and unrecognized ones. This hierarchy determined the similarly simple and rigid stricture of the artistic process for several decades.

In keeping with this hierarchy the official system of values was formed which determined, in turn, the priorities in the kinds of art, subjects and genres, motifs, characters and heroes. During these decades (to the middle of the 1950s) the repertory of themes and subjects in painting was strictly regimented. Huge canvases of official content were then fashionable eulogizing people's love for their leader and the enormous accomplishments of Stalin and his associates.

The Russian Museum, like many others, possesses quite a representative collection of art of the totalitarian age. But the collection amassed in the museum allows us to show the art of the period and the atmosphere of the age not only in its official version known to contemporaries from the pages of Soviet art magazines, exhibitions, art books, posters and picture postcards.

BORIS KUSTODIEV. 1878–1927
Merchant's Wife At Tea. 1918
Oil on canvas. 120 x 120

Art of the 1930s–1950s was not just the period of official portraits showing "the leaders' faces lacking personality" or huge canvases painted by a "shock-brigade method" and giant monuments seemingly arrested in their stately magnificence. The powerful traditions of Russian Realism were still alive, and there existed a fine art school from which, by the way, came out many eminent masters active in the 1960s–1980s. With their names is associated the so-called "Austere Style", which emerged primarily due to Khrushchev's "thaw" in the 1960s.

A huge amount of works produced by Alexander Deineka (1899–1969), Alexei Pakhomov (1900–1973), Vladimir Lebedev (1891–1967), Alexander Samokhvalov (1894–1971) and many other artists in the 1920s show intense efforts of the post-revolutionary artists to create art understandable to those who controlled it now.

Even in those years, however, the museum not only preserved the works by masters of the "classical" avant-garde of the 1900s–1920s, who were driven away from everywhere, but even acquired whenever possible works by artists who were "out of law" and pinned the label of "formalists". Works by many of them were kept in the museum's reserves for a long time without ever being showed or published.

An important source for augmenting the museum's collection of Russian art of the twentieth century were always art exhibitions. However, from 1932 onwards the activities related to the replenishment of the collections were rigidly limited by the ideological precepts.

Only in the middle of the 1950s a certain tolerance in the prohibitive policy could be observed. It was in this period that a large collection of works by Malevich officially became the property of the museum. During the same years the museum's collection was enriched with a large number of works by Kuzma Petrov-Vodkin. In the subsequent years the museum continued to augment its collection despite a negative attitude of the official authorities to avant-garde art.

BORIS GRIGORYEV. 1886–1939
Portrait of Vsevolod Meyerhold. 1916
Oil on canvas. 247 x 168

NATHAN ALTMAN. 1889–1970
Portrait of Anna Akhmatova. 1914
Oil on canvas. 123 x 103.2

VLADIMIR TATLIN. 1885–1953
Sailor. 1911
Tempera on canvas. 71.5 x 71.5

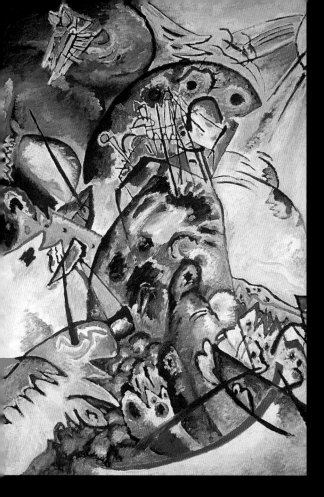

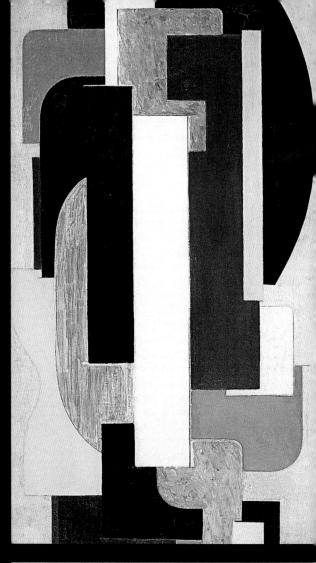

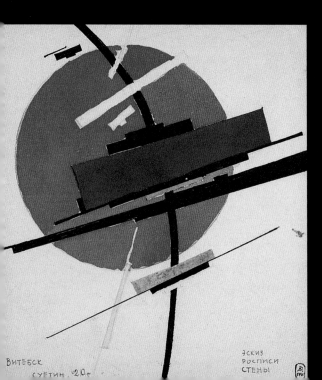

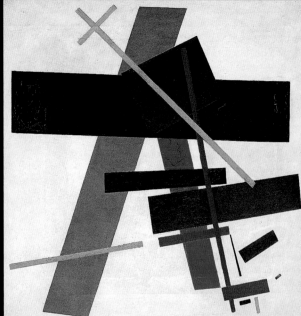

ВИТЕБСК
СУЕТИН. 20г.

ЭСКИЗ
РОСПИСИ
СТЕНЫ

WASSILY KANDINSKY
1866–1944
Blue Comb. 1917
Oil on canvas.133 x 104

VLADIMIR LEBEDEV
1891–1967
Cubism. 1922
Oil on canvas. 108 x 69

NIKOLAI SUETIN. 1897–1954
Sketch for wall decoration Vitebsk. 1920
Coloured ink on paper. 20.3 x 18.2

KASIMIR MALEVICH. 1878–1935
Suprematism. 1915–1916
Oil on canvas. 80.5 x 81

BORIS KOROLEV. 1885–1963
The Articulation of Forms of the Human Body. 1922
Plaster of Paris. 131.5 x 42 x 50

ALEXANDER RODCHENKO. 1891–1956
Red and Yellow. 1918(?)
Oil on canvas. 90 x 62

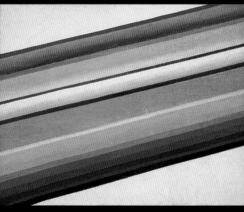

A normal art process slowly began to revive only in the 1960s. The Russian Museum acquired in this period many works by masters of different trends. This process continues to this day. One can see in the museum's display rooms now examples of art of the underground movement which was formed during the last Soviet decades. It was difficult to collect this kind of works — too many artists have been scattered around the world. Too many even in terms of the twentieth century when Russia pushed out one wave of emigration after another with a thoughtless generosity. But as the Bible says, "The wind goeth towards the south, and turneth about unto the north; it whirlieth about continually, and the wind returneth again according to his circuits." So the names and works of those without whom the panorama of the Russian art life of the 1970s and 1980s would be

incomplete are coming back to Russia. This period is well illustrated, for instance, in the works presented as a gift to the museum by
the well-known German art collectors Peter and Irena Ludwig.
"The Ludwig Museum within the Russian Museum" arranget in
the Marble Palace is destined to arouse in the viewer a sense of
the overall context of the Russian art school without which the
true existence of present-day national art is hardly conceivable.

Our notion of history is similar to the thickness of oceanic
water — the deeper into the centuries, the lesser movement is
noticeable; the closer to the present, the more tangible is the clash-
ing of currents. And as for today's surface, it is covered with waves
which make everything unsteady and vacillating. In the same way
not everything in twentieth-century art has become settled as yet.
Many years are to pass before everything would be arranged in
classificatory cells, a steady system of landmarks and definitions.
As for present-day art, the museum collects today both works executed in a traditional manner and those by avant-garde artists.

It can be said with certainty that the collection amassed in the
Russian Museum is sufficiently comprehensive and varied to give
the visitor an opportunity to build up a detailed and objective picture of the development of Russian art from the beginning of the
second millennium to the present day.

ÀLEXANDER LABAS. 1900–1983
The Plane Ant-20 "Maxim Gorky". 1934
Oil on canvas. 155.5 x 199

YURY KUGACH. Born 1917
VASILY NECHITAILO. 1915–1980
VICTOR TSYPLAKOV. 1915–1986
Long Live the Great Stalin! 1950
Oil on canvas. 351 x 525

ARKADY PLASTOV. 1893–1972
Midday. 1961
Oil on canvas. 174 x 231

THE PALACES
OF THE RUSSIAN MUSEUM

The Stroganov Palace

1753. Architect Francesco Bartolomeo Rastrelli

The Marble Palace

1768–85. Architect Antonio Rinaldi

The Mikhailovsky
(Engineers') Castle

1796–1800. Architects Vasily Bazhenov
and Vincenzo Brenna

The Stroganov Palace is the oldest building in the complex of palaces of the Russian Museum. It is located at the corner of Nevsky Prospect and the Moika River Embankment. The palace was erected in 1753 by the court architect Bartolomeo Francesco Rastrelli (1700–1771). The best of his works — the Smolny Convent, the Winter and the Stroganov Palaces — mark the culmination of the Russian Baroque, colourful and different from its Western counterpart. The palace was the property of many generations of the Stroganovs — an old rich and aristocratic family which largely contributed to Russia's glory by its exploits.

The eminent Italian painter Giuseppe Valeriani took part in the decoration of the palace alongside numerous sculptors, wood carvers and guilders. His ceiling painting *Telemachus on Olympus* decorates the Large Ballroom to this day. By the efforts of its owners, the "Stroganov palazzo" was turned into an abode of the Muses, a repository of various artistic collections. A large contribution in this respect was made by the most famous representative of the family, Count Alexander Stroganov, the Marshal of the Moscow Nobility, Chief Chamberlain of the Court and President of the Academy of Arts. At the turn of the eighteenth and nineteenth centuries Andrei Voronikhin, assisted by Fiodor Demertsov, made for him a radical alteration of the design of the palace's interiors. Voronikhin replaced the former private apartments with a series of new magnificent rooms and halls, in particular, the eastern suite consisting of the Mineralogical Study, Library and

the Study of Physics. The most remarkable room in the enfilade was the Picture Gallery called later the "soul of the Stroganov mansion" by Alexander Benois. For Count Alexander Stroganov's son, Pavel, Voronikhin decorated a series of rooms, including the Little Drawing Room and the Little Library.

After the revolution of 1917 the palace was nationalized and in 1919–31 it functioned as a museum of everyday life of the past. In 1929 by the Soviet Government issued a decree on the liquidation of all the collections from the palace, and this decision proved to be detrimental for the state of the historical edifice. The holdings were

View of the Stroganov Palace from the Police Bridge. 1840s
Coloured lithograph after a drawing by Joseph Charlemagne

ALEXANDER VARNECK
Portrait of Alexander Stroganov. 1814

JEAN-LAURENT MOSNIER
Portrait of Count Pavel Stroganov. 1808

JULES MAYBLUM
The Green Dining-Room in the Stroganov Palace
1863–65
Watercolour

The Corner Hall (The State Dinner-Room)

Detail of the painted decoration of the Arabesque Hall

The Picture Gallery. 1901
Photograph

View of the Stroganov Palace from the Moika River

distributed among different museums and some of them disappeared with no trace. In the 1930s the palace was occupied by a military organization which closed the doors of the palace even for specialists in history.

Only in 1989, after a transfer of the Stroganov Palace to the Russian Museum, its revival has begun. Several state rooms are already opened for visitors and displays are arranged in them.

The Marble Palace is a remarkable architectural monument dating from the second half of the eighteenth century. Even its contemporaries evaluated it as the "only one of its kind".

Catherine the Great, who wanted to erect the palace as a gift to Count Grigory Orlov, entrusted its construction to the Italian architect Antonio Rinaldi (1709–1794). The work began in 1768 to continue for seventeen years. The basic material used in the decoration of the building were varicoloured marbles and granites, hence its name.

On the death of Count Grigory Orlov Catherine the Great bought the palace from his successors and presented it in 1796 to her grandson, Grand Duke Konstantin Pavlovich. In 1832 Emperor Nicholas I gave the Marble Palace to his second son, Grand Duke Konstantin Nikolayevich. The court architect Alexander Briullov carried out a major reconstruction of the palace. The architect redesigned the interiors of the rooms and halls using the motifs of the Late Renaissance, Gothic, Rococo and Classicism.

In 1888 the palace became the property of Grand Duke Konstantin Konstantinovich, known mainly as an eminent poet of the Silver Age (he signed his works with the pseudonym *K.R.*). The English Study, the Gothic Music Drawing Room and the Lower Library were de-

signed for him. Today visitors are admitted to some of the interiors.

Between 1919 and 1936 the palace housed the Russian Academy of the History of Material Culture. In 1937 the rooms of the Marble Palace were used for exhibitions of the Leningrad Branch of the Lenin Central Museum. The new use of the rooms resulted in losses of the architectural decor of the first-floor interiors. Only the State Staircase and the Marble Hall were left intact. The centre of the ceiling above the State Staircase is adorned with *The Judgement of Paris* painted in the eighteenth-century by the artist I. Christ. Seven kinds of Greek, Italian, Ural, Karelian and Siberian marbles were used for the decor of the Marble Hall. The hall is embellished with bas-reliefs created by the sculptors Fedot Shubin and Mihail Kozlovsky and with the ceiling painting *The Triumph of Venus* by Stefano Torelli.

In January 1992 the Marble Palace became the property of the Russian Museum. Nowadays it houses permanent displays "The Ludwig Museum within the Russian Museum" and "Western European Artists in Russia"; temporary exhibitions of contemporary artists are also arranged there.

View of the Marble Palace from the Neva 1840s
Lithograph after a drawing by Joseph Charlemagne

STEFANO TORELLI
Portrait of Count Grigory Orlov. Before 1763

MIKHAIL RUNDALTSEV
Portrait of Grand Duke Konstantin Konstantinovich

View of the Marble Palace from the Neva

The State Staircase

The inner courtyard of the Marble Palace

The Marble Hall

The Marble Palace

The Mikhailovsky Castle, which combines the features of a medieval castle and a secular European eighteenth-century palace, was the state residence of Emperor Paul I. It was named after Archangel Michael, the heavenly patron of the Romanov House.

The history of the castle's design and construction involves many vague details. After his return from the famous travel abroad in 1784, Grand Duke Pavel Petrovich (the future Emperor Paul I) began to think about an architectural solution of his future palace. He engaged the Swiss artist and architect Henri François Viollier (1750–1829) as his assistant. Later Vasily Bazhenov (1737–1799) and the Italian Vincenzo Brenna (1745–1820) participated in this work. After the death of Catherine the Great in 1796, on his accession, Paul I received an opportunity to start the long-awaited construction. The work was carried out very quickly and on 8 November 1800 the castle was consecrated.

The majestic building was put up on an island — the castle was separated from the mainland on the two sides by the Fontanka and the Moika, and canals were dug out to protect the southern and western façades. The Emperor set up in front of the palace the equestrian statue of Peter the Great created earlier, in the 1740s, by the well-known sculptor Carlo Bartolomeo Rastrelli.

The interiors of the palace, which combined the features of a living residence and a museum of ancient, Western European and Russian art, were marked by opulence and majesty. Along the perimeter of the inner courtyard there runs a suite of long state rooms — the Hall of Antiques, the Galleries of Raphael, Laocoön and Arabesques — which were filled with unique works of art. The state halls of the palace were painted by Johann Jacob Mettenleiter, Antonio Vighi, Pietro and Giovanni Battista Scotti and Franciszek Smuglewicz.

The Mikhailovsky Palace served to its owner only for forty days. During the night of 12 March 1801 Paul I was murdered in his bedroom as a result of a conspiracy.

In the early 1820s the edifice began to house the Main Engineering College (in 1823 the building was renamed the Engineers' Castle). Many well-known people, including the great writer Fiodor Dostoyevsky, studied there.

The college was located in the building until the 1960s, then the castle-palace began to house the Central Naval Library which still occupies the state rooms. The rest of the palace was given to designing and research institutions.

In March 1995 the building was handed over to the Russian Museum. The permanent exhibition "Russian Formal Portraiture" was arranged in the restored rooms; the palace is also the venue for numerous art exhibitions.

FEODOR ALEXEYEV
View of the Mikhailovsky Castle from the Fontanka River. Ca 1800

STEPAN SHCHUKIN
Portrait of Paul I

Monogram of Emperor Paul I on the northern façade of the Mikhailovsky Castle

View of the Mikhailovsky Castle from the Fontanka River

Monument to Peter the Great in front of the southern façade of the Mikhailovsky Castle

The chancel of the Church of the Archangel Michael

The Hall of Ancient Sculpture

The Russian Museum

A Pictorial Guide

Foreword by Vladimir Gusev
Selection and text by Vladimir Gusev and Yevgeniya Petrova
Translated from the Russian by Valery Fateyev. Designed by Nikolai Kutovoi
Photographs by Pavel Demidov, Vladimir Dorokhov, Georgy Shablovsky, Oleg Trubsky and Vasily Vorontsov
Edited by Irina Kharitonova and Irina Ivova. Proof-reading by Irina Dubrovskaya
Computer layout by Yelena Morozova and Nina Sokolova

ISBN 5-93893-041-3